MONUMENT

TO

THE MEMORY

OF

HENRY CLAY.

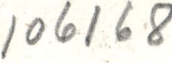

"He was a MAN, take him for all in all,
WE shall not look upon his like again."

"I WOULD RATHER BE RIGHT, THAN BE PRESIDENT."

PHILADELPHIA:
DUANE RULISON, 33 SOUTH THIRD STREET.
CINCINNATI:
W. A. CLARKE, 119 WALNUT STREET.
1858.

Entered according to Act of Congress, in the year 1856, by
WM. A. CLARKE,
In the Clerk's Office of the District Court of the United States, for the Southern District of Ohio.

STEREOTYPED BY
D. HILLS & CO.,
141 Main St., Cincinnati.

PREFACE.

The object of the present work is two-fold. First, to present in a condensed form a complete Life, and the most important Speeches of Henry Clay; and secondly, to collect, in a form adapted to their preservation, the Eulogies called forth by the death of the great statesman, together with an account of the Obsequies attending his burial.

In respect to the first object, it may be said, that the field has already been occupied. In reply, we say that, although the works which have appeared from time to time, and especially the large volumes of Colton, have given us nearly all the information which we can hope to obtain, whether in regard to the public or private life of HENRY CLAY, yet that they all, and especially those which we have designated, labor under the disadvantage of being too large and too costly for popular circulation.

Now, such was the affectionate admiration with which HENRY CLAY was regarded, while living, that we believe thousands will hail with satisfaction the appearance of a volume like this, in which it has been the aim to unite accuracy in the statement of facts, with a clear delineation of the marked features of CLAY's public and private character. The Biographic part claims, moreover, to be something more than a mere abridgment or compilation. It aspires to the dignity of an original portraiture.

In the Selections from CLAY's speeches, the rule observed was this; to present the political opinions of the great leader in his own words, rendering him, thus, as far as possible, the author of his own political biography. To this end, extracts have been made to convey, not always so much an impression of the beauty and force of his diction, as of the peculiar sentiments which he entertained, the form in which he held them, and the arguments with which he defended them. They have been arranged with express reference to their biographic value.

In regard to the contents of the latter part of the volume, we need only say, that they can not but have a value while the memory of HENRY CLAY shall live, as indicating the mode in which a mighty nation gave expression to its grief, at the loss of its favorite son.

The volume then as a whole, we trust, will vindicate its pretensions, notwithstanding defects which, doubtless, exist in it, to be considered truly a monument to the memory of HENRY CLAY.

PARIS, KENTUCKY *March* 1, 1857.

CONTENTS.

THE LIFE OF HENRY CLAY.

CHAPTER I.

What constitutes a true monument—The best position for estimating a public man—Men have often a distinct private and public character—Which their true character—Essentials of a perfect biography.................................... 9

CHAPTER II.

Birth and parentage—Death of his father—Its probable influence upon his after history—Significance of the incident of "the mill-boy of the Slashes"—His schooling—A foolish opinion, that genius does not need education—What education means—Whether HENRY CLAY, in this sense, was educated—He enters Mr. Denny's store—Obtains a situation in the clerk's office, at Richmond—Attracts the attention of Chancellor Wythe—Studies law with Attorney-General Brooke—Is admitted to the bar—Result of the influence upon him of such men as Wythe and Brooke—He engages in a rhetorical society—Inquiry, whether greatness is the offspring of circumstances—CLAY moves to Kentucky..,............ 13

CHAPTER III.

Mr. CLAY's modest opinion of himself—His competitors in Kentucky—The debating club—Kentucky people—Alien and Sedition Laws—Mr. CLAY's success in law—His marriage—His election to the Legislature—To the Senate of the United States—Aaron Burr—Legislature of Kentucky again—Duel with Humphrey Marshall—His abilities in the State Legislature............................ 21

CHAPTER IV.

Senate of the United States again—Policy of our country—Mr CLAY advocates protection of domestic manufactures—Opposes a United States Bank—His activity in bringing about a war with England—Declaration of war... 35

CONTENTS.

CHAPTER V.

Early disasters of the war—Subsequent successes—Negotiations for peace—Ghent—Mr. CLAY a Commissioner—Terms of the treaty—Mr. CLAY visits England—United States Bank—Mr. CLAY's change of views—What constitutes true Political Economy—Compensation bill—CLAY is obliged to canvass his State—South American independence. 44

CHAPTER VI.

Mr. CLAY is offered the post of Minister to Russia—Also, a place in the Cabinet—Advocates internal improvements—Mr. CLAY the father of a policy and a party—The character and services of the Whig party—Seminole war—The conduct of Jackson............ 54

CHAPTER VII.

Mr. CLAY as a "pacificator"—Missouri desires admission—Violent agitation of slavery—The Compromise—The efforts of Mr. CLAY... 60

CHAPTER VIII.

Candidates for the Presidency in 1824—No election by the people—Mr. CLAY's influence given to Mr. Adams—Charge of corruption—Mr. Kremer of Pennsylvania—Revival of the charge by Jackson—More trouble—A Duel with Randolph............................ 66

CHAPTER IX.

The Tariff of 1824—Question as to the expediency of a Protective tariff—Difference between theory and practice—Unpopularity of the protective system at the South—Nullification—Mr. CLAY introduces his Compromise Tariff, and harmony is restored................. 71

CHAPTER X.

Mr. CLAY is again defeated as a candidate for the Presidency—CLAY and Jackson as rival leaders—Removal of the Deposits by the President—Mr. CLAY's indignant opposition—Resolution of censure—The Cherokees—Lavish expenditure—The expunging resolution—The Sub-treasury bill—Dawning of better times 85

CHAPTER XI.

Enthusiasm of 1840—Extra session of Congress—Death of Harrison—Defection of Tyler—Grief of Mr. CLAY, at the subversion of his cherished hopes—He advocates a tariff, designed for Protection—Resigns his seat—His farewell to the Senate..................... 97

CHAPTER XII.

Mr. Clay is again candidate for the Presidency, and suffers renewed defeat—Sorrow of his friends—War with Mexico—Acquisition of Territory—Embarrassing questions—Danger to the Union—Mr. Clay accepts a seat in the Senate—His heroic efforts to quiet the distraction of his country—It is the Chieftain's last battle—Disease advances—His death—His abilities as a statesman and orator—His characteristics as a man.................................. 116

SPEECHES, ETC.

On Domestic Manufactures. In the Senate of the United States, April 6, 1810.. 131

On Renewing the Charter of the First Bank of the United States. In the Senate of the United States, 1811........................ 137

On the United States Bank Question. Address to his Constituents at Lexington, June 3, 1816....................................... 153

On Internal Improvement. In the House of Representatives, March 13, 1818... 161

On the Greek Revolution. In the House of Representatives, January 20, 1824... 172

On American Industry. In the House of Representatives, March 30 and 31, 1824... 181

Address to La Fayette. House of Representatives, December 10, 1824. 205

The American System, etc. Delivered at Cincinnati, August 3, 1830. 207

On the Public Lands Bill. In the Senate of the United States December 29, 1835 239

Petitions for the Abolition of Slavery. In the Senate of the United States, February 7, 1839.. 248

On the Bank Veto. In reply to the Speech of Mr. Rives, of Virginia, on the Executive Message containing the President's Objection to the Bank Bill. In the Senate of the United States, August 19, 1841. 263

On his Retirement to Private Life. At Lexington, Kentucky, June 9, 1842... 271

On the Compromise Measures, Reported by the Committee of Thirteen. In the Senate of the United States, May 13, 1850.......... 286

Address to Kossuth. December, 1851............................ 317

EULOGIES, ETC.

Eulogy of Joseph R. Underwood, of Kentucky.................... 321
Eulogy of Lewis Cass, of Michigan 330
Eulogy of Robert M. T. Hunter, of Virginia...................... 334
Eulogy of John P. Hale, of New Hampshire...................... 338
Eulogy of Jeremiah Clemens, of Alabama........................ 341
Eulogy of James Cooper, of Pennsylvania......................... 344
Eulogy of William H. Seward, of New York...................... 349
Eulogy of George W. Jones, of Iowa. 356
Eulogy of Walter Brooke, of Mississippi........................ 359
    Delivered in the United States Senate.

Eulogy of John C. Breckinridge, of Kentucky 363
Eulogy of Presley Ewing, of Kentucky........................... 371
Eulogy of John S. Caskie, of Virginia............................ 375
Eulogy of Joseph R. Chandler, of Pennsylvania................... 377
Eulogy of Thomas H. Bayly, of Virginia.......................... 382
Eulogy of Abraham W. Venable, of North Carolina................ 385
Eulogy of Solomon G. Haven, of New York state.................. 391
Eulogy of James Brooks, of New York city....................... 393
Eulogy of Charles J. Faulkner, of Virginia....................... 396
Eulogy of Samuel W. Parker, of Indiana.......................... 403
Eulogy of Meredith P. Gentry, of Tennessee...................... 406
Eulogy of Richard J. Bowie, of Maryland......................... 407
Eulogy of Thomas Y. Walsh, of Maryland......................... 409
    Delivered in the House of Representatives.

Eulogy of John J. Crittenden, of Kentucky 413
    Delivered at Louisville, Kentucky, September 29, 1852.

Eulogy of Henry W. Hilliard, of Alabama........................ 437
    Delivered before the Citizens of Montgomery, Alabama, September, 1852.

Eulogy of Alexander K. M'Clung, of Mississippi.................. 470
    Delivered in the Hall of the House of Rep. of the State of Mississippi, Oct. 11, 1852.

Obsequies... 489
Sermon by Rev. C. M. Butler, D. D.............................. 491
Lines by George D. Prentice.................................... 515

THE

LIFE OF HENRY CLAY.

CHAPTER I.

INTRODUCTORY.

What constitutes a true monument—The best position for estimating a public man—Men have often a distinct private and public character—Which their true character—Essentials of a perfect biography.

In any high sense, there is but one thing which men may call a monument. The skillfully-chiseled marble of the churchyard can be purchased, as well by money, as by merit. The canvas, glowing with the semblance of life, is, how often, a monument rather of the genius of the artist, than of the forgotten dead, whose features it perpetuates. Triumphal arches and pyramids even, however deeply and strongly they may be founded, change at last to ruinous heaps, or are intrusted, in vain, with the names of their builders and the records of the deeds which they commemorate.

Nevertheless, greatness has its enduring monument. But that monument is erected by itself. Laid sometimes, indeed, in the blood and tears of suffering humanity, built up amid the sighs of lacerated bosoms, and crowned with the execrations of a long posterity; but sometimes based upon the noblest impulses of a noble heart, erected every part of it to bless and adorn humanity, and completed amid shouts of gratitude, or those more expressive tokens of affection—a nation's tears.

When we speak then of a monument, commemorative of HENRY CLAY, we mean not the marble which may cover his moldering remains, nor any imposing columns, which men may hereafter erect in their places of public resort. We mean, his own great character; his matchless will; the thoughts which he entertained; the words which he spoke; his large sagacity; and that larger patriotism, which achieved for his country continued peace and prosperity—for himself, a place, like that of a household idol, in every American heart.

To the life of HENRY CLAY we must look for his monument. It is obvious, then, that his life should be so presented, as to make what we may call, its historic impression.

The particular phase of mind, or social temper, which is best known to a great man's familiar friends, bears, often, no higher relation to his character in its completeness, than the peculiar forms of rock or foliage, which come, more immediately, under the observation of the dwellers at the foot of the mountain, bear to the dimensions and outline of the whole mass. When *great* objects are to be estimated, nearness of position can not always be accounted a favorable circumstance. The work of the biographer, resembles, somewhat, that of the engraver, who must, with a few bold and discriminating lines, present what is individual and peculiar in the features to be delineated; or perhaps, better yet, we may compare it with those works of the sculptor which are to stand at a distance, or upon an elevation. The finer details are left comparatively untouched, while the peculiar outlines are executed strongly.

The biographer must present, as nearly as possible, the impression which the greatness that he describes made upon its own age, but it must be ever with this discrimination, he must present each striking action or characteristic, not in the light of its temporary importance, but of its historic permanence and value. This, to a cotemporary biographer, is a task of no small difficulty. Hence, it often happens, that greatness receives its best estimate years after men are familiar with it, except in its results. The partiality of affection, the contempt, which is said to spring up in little minds from familiarity, and the prejudices of enmity, are alike fatal to the truth of biography.

The household friends of Clay ; the farmers and shopkeepers, with whom he had frequent dealings; and the enemies, who persecuted him with their slanders, would, severally, be unqualified to draw with correctness his portrait. Yet, it can not be denied, that the biographer, who lives near the time of the character which he describes, possesses important advantages over those who come after him. The many little incidents, illustrative of character, which live their short life in the memory of friends, serve often, as a sufficient clue to mysteries of public conduct, which the subsequent historian might seek in vain to decipher. Things which might otherwise be accounted trifles, are, in this way, not unfrequently invested with no small significance. Private details may be regarded as scattered rays, valuable in proportion to the quantity of light which they can throw upon the main object; this, in historical characters, being not the private but the public and official conduct. It would, indeed, do great injustice to many, perhaps to most of those who have figured largely in the world's estimation, to depict them, mainly as they have appeared in social life. Men often bear what would seem two distinct characters—so distinct as even to amount to an apparent contradiction. The question with the biographer, in such a case, must be, which will give the most correct impression ? which represents, most truly, the effective character ? Charles II sought, in disguise, the acquaintance of the author of Hudibras, thinking that he should find him a most facetious fellow ; but so great was the king's disappointment, that he was led to pronounce him a stupid blockhead, and to declare it to be impossible, that he could ever have written so witty a book. Tradition affirms, of Shakspeare, that after obtaining a competency from his dramatic works, he settled down quietly upon a farm, varying the monotony of his life by an occasional visit to the nearest market town, to execute small commissions for himself and his neighbors. What idea of the immortal dramatist should we now possess, had it been left to one of those neighbors to transmit his personal impressions of the "chiel amang" them!

The elegant Addison, and the genial Lamb, are said to have been reserved in general society. In such cases, it is evident which phase of character must be presented, unless injustice would be done.

Yet, even more, in the case of statesmen, must historic faithfulness be regarded, because they leave no such oft-perused records of themselves, from which to correct mistaken impressions.

The highest form of character which a man has ever developed, even if that display of power has been but short and occasional, is a more just index of what he is, and of what he can do, than his intermediate periods, though disproportionately long, of mediocrity and indolence. For in this only does he vindicate his title to greatness, and render himself an object of possible interest to posterity. Keeping this fact in view, it will be evident, that the more clearly the character described is made to stand out in its individuality, the more perfectly the reader is made to feel a direct approach to it, the better will the ends of biography be answered.

The day has forever passed by, in which history may be a dry catalogue of facts. Men put away contemptuously the skeleton, and demand the action and glow of life. This has evidently widened the province of biography, for to convey an adequate impression of a man's effective force, the history of his time must be displayed, the circumstances which made him what he was, and, those more hidden things, the probable motives of his conduct.

Where so much is implied, the reader will be considerate, it is hoped, if he encounter occasional mistakes and misapprehensions.

BIRTH PLACE OF HENRY CLAY.

CHAPTER II.

Birth and parentage—Death of his father—Its probable influence upon his after history—Significance of the incident of "the mill-boy of the Slashes"—His schooling—A foolish opinion, that genius does not need education—What education means—Whether HENRY CLAY, in this sense, was educated—He enters Mr. Denny's store—Obtains a situation in the clerk's office, at Richmond—Attracts the attention of Chancellor Wythe—Studies law with Attorney—General Brooke—Is admitted to the bar—Result of the influence upon him of such men as Wythe and Brooke—He engages in a rhetorical society—Inquiry, whether greatness is the offspring of circumstances—CLAY moves to Kentucky.

VIRGINIA, if asked, like the Roman matron, to display her jewels, could point, with an equal maternal pride, to her many illustrious sons. It is not her least occasion for boasting that she gave birth to HENRY CLAY.

The future statesman was born April 12th, 1777, in Hanover County, in a neighborhood called the Slashes. His parentage may be denominated humble. His father was a Baptist clergyman, deriving from his salary, doubtless, but a bare subsistence for a somewhat numerous family. Of the incidents of his earliest years, we have no record of any kind. It would not be difficult to draw an imaginary picture, which we might safely pronounce true in some of its features. We have no reason, and no occasion to suppose that his infancy was distinguished by any thing unusual. It is a fertile fancy, which goes back to the cradle, to find indications of the coming greatness.

Yet, we are not to disregard the providences, which direct our course of life, even from its outset. Events which seem the merest accidents, often hold in their keeping our whole subsequent history.

The death of HENRY CLAY's father, while the son was yet but four years of age, may have been to him such an event. The burden of so young a family, thrown upon the mother, would cause her to rear her children with a view to their self-dependence, and prompt her to seek for them, as early as possible, situations in which they might make their own subsistence.

In fact, one of the earliest known incidents of HENRY CLAY's life, the source of no small enthusiasm, and of a name which became the rallying cry of more than one political contest—the story of the mill-boy of the Slashes—indicates that we are to look thus far back, if we would penetrate to the hidden springs of his mighty self-reliance.

The frequent pilgrimages to "Mrs. Darricott's mill, upon Pamunkey River," by the awkward lad astride of the meal-bag, upon the pony, guided by its rope bridle, probably indicated to the neighbors nothing more than filial faithfulness; yet, all that time, though unconsciously even to himself, the seeds were sowing, the ripened harvest of which was gathering in when he took his seat, as presiding officer, in the legislative halls of his country; when further on, his tones commanded respect on that floor, where to be accorded, it is necessary, in a measure, to be commanded; and when, most of all, his words, now of entreaty, now of warning, and anon, as if of command, were heard pleading, first with the South, and again with the North, until both laid by their anger, appeased by the magic of his earnestness and his eloquence.

It may seem fanciful to some, to go thus far back for "the hidings of his power." But let it be considered, that we take the incident, not so much for what it is in itself as for the evidence which it gives, of an early, manly grapple with real labor, and real difficulties. We discern in it the beginning of a habit—and what significance does not that word convey—a habit of self-dependence, ready to ripen into every fruit of excellence. To magnify too highly the effect of such early influences is hardly possible.

Viewed in this light, we venture the assertion, that there was a deeper reason for selecting the incident of the mill-boy of the Slashes, to construct from it a name for the nation's idol, than was comprehended by the thousands who made it their rallying shout.

Of school instruction, HENRY CLAY, apparently, received scarcely any thing. Mention is made of three years' tuition in a log school-house, under the care of Peter Deacon, a convivial Englishman. His whole *curriculum*, as they say in universities, amounted only to reading, writing, and "arithmetic, as far as Practice." Our fathers had not then bestirred themselves in the matter of common schools. But, had the advantages of the period been ten-fold what they were, there is occasion to doubt whether, in the destitute condition of his mother, HENRY CLAY would have been able greatly to avail himself of them. He at least, we may believe, would not have been in the way of becoming what is termed, "an elegant classic." We never can be brought to depreciate the advantages of a thorough education, but all honor, we say, to the man who, despite of the want of it, can make his way to "the high places of the earth."

A foolish opinion is extensively prevalent, that greatness does not need, or that it disdains, the usual toilsome course to excellence. Indolent school-boys and dissipated college lads are prone to quote the example of HENRY CLAY, of Patrick Henry, and of Daniel Webster even, to justify their idleness, and to prove, by a curious process of logic, that they are thus giving indications of genius. The great men, whose names they are guilty of thus taking in vain, would be the last to give their voices in confirmation of such a conclusion. The silly error has grown out of a misapprehension of what is implied in the term education. It is generally thought to mean an infusing into the mind of a certain amount of information, classical, mathematical, technical, or historical. But, to think thus, is to confound the end with the means. Every kind of information existent may have a tendency to educate, but of itself, can not constitute the work. That man is *educated* who, by whatever means, has made his powers available, and he is best educated, who can make his talents effective to their highest extent.

Now it is usually thought, and doubtless wisely, that a severe course of classical and mathematical training will best effect this result—will, in other words, render a man most perfectly the master of his powers. In saying this, we include the expansion of mind, which naturally comes from a wide range of information, and the habitual, manly exercise of thought. If now, any other course than that of the university, will be productive of equal results, then that process, whatever its nature, may be called education. While, on the other hand, if the *curriculum* of the university has failed in this, its legitimate end, the failure is total so far as the term education can be applied to it.

Viewing the matter in this light, it is more than doubtful, whether HENRY CLAY can be said to have been destitute of early education. Although he was not, in the ordinary sense, a student, during the fourteen years of his life preceding his entrance as a clerk into Mr. Richard Denny's store, in Richmond, nor, we may add, at any time subsequent, yet in that effectiveness, which we have shown to be implied in education, he might all the time have been making rapid proficiency. He, we may at least believe, judging from his experiences as a mill-boy, was learning those practical lessons which would prove invaluable to him, when afterward called upon to undertake larger work, and encounter real difficulties. He was training his faculties for that prompt decision, in which the most admirable and learned theorizers are often deficient, but which is always indispensable to the man of business, and most of all, to the politician and statesman. We do not know but that Providence, in its disposition of the early life of HENRY CLAY, and of so many others who have come up from the humble ranks of society, arranged every thing with an obvious reference to the highest effectiveness of their after career. Their history is, at all events, no proclamation hung out to indolence and stupidity.

HENRY CLAY did not long remain behind Mr. Denny's counter, tying packages, and compounding simples for sick children. His new stepfather, Captain Watkins, had somewhat higher aspirations for him. Through the influence of a friend, he obtained for him a situation in the office of Peter Tinsley, Esq., clerk of the High Court of Chancery. His awkward manners and his tall form, set off, not to the best advantage, by a suit of homespun, excited at first, the ridicule of his fellow-clerks, but upon better acquaintance their laughter was made to yield to sincere respect for his abilities and worth.

His fortunes can not be thought to have advanced, as yet, very high, though certainly, at this point they begin to mend. He is, for the first time, definitely upon the road which is to conduct him to renown. Between the mill-boy of the Slashes or the compounder of drugs, and the leader upon either floor of Congress, we can discover no particular relation, but the path from an office of law to the same high position, it is more easy to determine. The entrance into Mr. Tinsley's office we may consider the turning-point of his early history.

His advantages here were doubtless not very great, but he attracted the attention of Chancellor Wythe, and in that fact found new and wider prospects open before him. The chancellor engaged his services as an amanuensis, and, finding in him evidences of an inquiring mind, gave him access to his library. Daily familiarity with a dignified and cultivated man, like Chancellor Wythe, even if it never took the intimate form of companionship, could not fail to exert a powerful influence upon the young and plastic mind of CLAY; while the turn that his reading would receive, from the judicious counsel of one so capable of advising, could not fail to be to him of infinite service; the more so, because, not having enjoyed the advantages of early systematic training, his curiosity might have led him into many fruitless literary explorations. HENRY CLAY remained with the chancellor four years—years more pregnant with future results, we may believe, than any equal period of his previous life.

From this scene of his labors, he passed, at the instance of the chancellor, to the office of Robert Brooke, Esq., attorney-general of Virginia. With this gentleman he pursued the study of law, during one year, at the end of which time he was admitted to practice in the Virginia Court of Appeals. He was now twenty years of age, and there can be no doubt, that his intimate association during several preceding years with the most courtly gentlemen of Virginia, had gone far toward producing in the awkward youth, the dignity and gracefulness for which he was pre-eminent as a man; toward disciplining his powers for effective action, and infusing into his mind those elevated habits of thought, which constituted him the far-seeing and commanding statesman.

It is a fact worth relating in this connection, that he was active in the formation of a rhetorical society, which embraced some of the most refined and promising of the young men of Richmond, and that he was, if tradition may be relied upon, one of the most marked and brilliant of its members.

The early history of eloquent men is a curious commentary upon the oft-repeated assertion, that greatness is the offspring of circumstances. We can not leave the history of HENRY CLAY, where poverty and the struggle against disadvantages are about to give place, by rapid gradations, to competence and a nation's applause, without applying the test to what, we believe to be, in some measure a fallacy.

Men as great may, possibly, have lived in this country, as Webster, CLAY, Calhoun, Hamilton, and Jefferson, entirely unknown to fame, but we are not prepared to believe it. These men might, under some circumstances, have themselves remained unknown, but we are not quite prepared to believe that.

Circumstances, we doubt not, have prodigious weight, but at the best they furnish only the training and the field for exercise. They fail in what is most indispensable of all—they do not create the man. Otherwise, every emergency would find, not merely its few worthy leaders, but would produce a universal crop of greatness.

Let us see, for instance, how much HENRY CLAY owed to outward circumstances in the forming period of his life. He was born, then, in an humble lot—a condition from which it is said the most of greatness has sprung, because, more than any other, it tends to develop hardiness of character. Luxury, it is rightly said, enervates. Great advantages are often not valued. The want of them is the spur to activity.

To this it may be answered, that it is not remarkable that a humble station should have furnished the most numerous instances of greatness. The doctrine of probabilities would have indicated thus much, since by far the larger portion of the human race are in humble circumstances. To the rest of the argument, it may be said, if the humble birth and childhood of Clay were the sources of his strength, why are not the unnumbered thousands of like instances fruitful in such results.

We would not, in this, be thought guilty of unsaying what we have urged in the course of this chapter, in favor of practical and severe training. While we have magnified its value, we trust that we have done it with sufficient discrimination to be free from the charge of self-refutation.

A writer,* at once elegant and powerful, has expressed so forcibly the truth upon which we are insisting, that we can not forbear quoting a paragraph: "The greatness or smallness of a man is, in the most conclusive sense, determined for him at his birth, as strictly as it is determined for a fruit, whether it is to be a currant or an apricot. Education, favorable circumstances, resolution and industry, can do much; in a certain sense they do every thing; that is to say, they determine whether the poor apricot shall fall in the form of a green bead, blighted by an east wind, shall be trodden under foot, or whether it shall expand into tender pride, and sweet brightness of golden velvet. But, apricot out of currant, great man out of small, did never yet art or effort make, and in a general way, men have their excellence nearly fixed for them when they are born; a little cramped and frost-bitten on one side, a little sunburnt and fortune-spotted on the other, they reach, between good and evil chances, such size and taste as generally belong to the men of their caliber, and the small in their serviceable bunches, the great in their golden isolation, have, these no cause for regret, nor those for disdain."

Greatness, in truth, is indigenous to no soil. If born in the soul, it is safe to assert, that it will come out under every variety of training and circumstance, subject, perhaps, only to this condition, that its degree of development will depend, in a measure,

---

* Ruskin, Modern Painters, Vol. iii.

upon its opportunities for action. Look at Fox, the spoiled child of a luxurious father, rising, despite luxury, despite gaming, despite dissoluteness, into "the most brilliant and accomplished debater," in the language of Burke, "the world ever saw." See Pitt, from his infancy trained with reference to his future statesmanship, and declaiming, when a child, from a chair, to the guests at his father's dinner table. See Burke, coming up with the ordinary advantages of good classical training, and distancing them all. See Chatham, bred in luxury, and whom, more than any other CLAY resembles, bearing every thing down by the resistless storm of his eloquence; and then turn to Patrick Henry, sitting indolently upon a barrel-head in his grocery, and looking, although with no meaningless stare, upon the rude sports of his customers; to our CLAY, not the least among them, spending his earlier years in almost menial employment. The commentary upon greatness furnished by such varied circumstances may not, it would seem, be mistaken.

We have now traced the history of CLAY, so far as it is identified with Virginia. It was the place only of his birth and training. With his license in his pocket, he seeks fortune and fame in a new home, though, as it will appear, with modest expectations in respect to both. His history, except that portion of it which belongs to his whole country, is henceforward, identified with Kentucky.

CHAPTER III.

Mr. Clay's modest opinion of himself—His competitors in Kentucky—The debating club—Kentucky people—Alien and Sedition Laws—Mr. Clay's success in law—His marriage—His election to the Legislature—To the Senate of the United States—Aaron Burr—Legislature of Kentucky again—Duel with Humphrey Marshall—His abilities in the State Legislature.

In one of his discriminating essays, Hazlitt has discussed the question: "Whether genius is conscious of its powers?" "No really great man," he asserts, "ever thought himself so. The idea of greatness in the mind answers but ill to our knowledge, or to our ignorance of ourselves. No man is truly himself, but in the idea which others entertain of him. The mind, as well as the eye, 'sees not itself but by reflection from some other thing.'"

The opinion which Henry Clay entertained, concerning his own abilities and probable success, seems to corroborate the assertion of Hazlitt. In the course of a speech, at a banquet given him by his friends, June, 1842, upon occasion of his retirement to private life, he says:

"I obtained a license to practice the profession of law, from the judges of the Court of Appeals of Virginia, and established myself in Lexington, in 1797, without patrons, without the favor or countenance of the great or opulent, without the means of paying my weekly board, and in the midst of a bar uncommonly distinguished by eminent members.

"I remember how comfortable I thought I should be, if I could make one hundred pounds, Virginia money, per year, and with what delight I received the first fifteen shillings fee. My hopes were more than realized. I immediately rushed into a successful and lucrative practice."

(21)

This brief allusion, by HENRY CLAY himself, to his "start in life," serves the purpose of a complete and graphic picture. He has left the Old Dominion behind, with its stirring and classic memories. He has left the polished society of Richmond, in which remembrance of his early struggles with poverty might have imposed upon him an irksome constraint. He has left the learned bar, toward which, as having furnished him with his patrons and instructors, he might have looked with a deference too great for his future independence of character and mind. He has turned his steps, like so many of more aspiring ambition since that day, to the Great West. Whatever his dreams of success, they are yet too dim to be told to others, to be whispered even to himself. He has not yet felt within the kindling of that inspiration, which is to fascinate and subdue the hearts of his countrymen. He has not yet waked up to the consciousness, that he is possessed of any unusual power. He feels himself to be only plain HENRY CLAY, but just now deputy clerk, amanuensis, and law student. A bare support, in his new home, is the hight of his expectations.

His modesty seems even to have kept him from asking for admission to the Fayette bar, until he had given several months' additional attention to his legal studies. Though he had left the refinements of Virginia, he found that he was by no means beyond the pale of civilization, and that his opponents were to be something more than backwoodsmen. It is doubtful whether the bar of Fayette county was ever more ably represented. Lexington had appropriated to itself all that was most choice and vigorous in the talent of the State. Breckenridge, and Nicholas, and Brown, and Hughes, and Murray, were men from whom the palm of superiority could be wrested by no competitor, without a struggle.

They were also established in business and reputation, when the new and diffident candidate for wealth and honor entered the lists against them. But self-distrust still held him back. He could not persuade himself yet, to measure his strength with theirs. What he was reluctant to do, was, however, at last forced upon him, as it were, by accident. He had become a member of a debating club, but had never ventured to speak upon any question. One night, it is related, as the debate was about to close, he whispered to a neighbor, that something more, he thought, might be said upon the subject. The remark was eagerly caught at, as affording an opportunity for calling out the young stranger, and ascertaining what "stuff he was made of." The president delayed to put the question, and from every side the call was made for "CLAY." Half surprised into the discussion, and yet half eager for it, the young orator arose, blushing and confused. The first words which he stammered out were, "Gentlemen of the jury." This unpropitious beginning deepened his embarrassment. Again he exclaimed, "Gentlemen of the jury!" But his hearers were considerate. Their courtesy restored his composure. His ideas quickly became clear and well expressed. His enthusiasm became roused. An ingenuous pride, to thoroughly redeem his opening effort from the appearance of failure, which it first assumed, quickened his intellect and fired his emotions. Whatever credit, for abilities, his silent good sense might have acquired for him before, his success now took his audience by storm. Their surprise, delight and applause were unbounded. That was an auspicious evening to him. Thenceforward, he might regard his fortune as made. The expectations of the community were to be allies upon his side, and he himself had awaked to a consciousness of his power. The days when "fifteen shillings fees" were a source of delight, will now rush away to give place to a successful and lucrative practice.

To every class of mind, the gay and grave, the learned and the ignorant, there is something fascinating in the eloquence of highly wrought feeling. It arises, in part, from a love of excitement, natural to every human breast, and, in part, from admiration of a high display of power; that power seeming especially wonderful, which can, at will, alternately excite and subdue the varied feelings of a large assembly.

But perhaps none give themselves up so entirely to its fascination, as do the unlearned and uncritical. Unaccustomed to dissemble their emotions, impulsiveness becomes their ruling habit; and, with something of the simplicity of children, they yield themselves to the power of the orator. Eloquence is regarded by them, with more enthusiasm, perhaps, than even military exploits, by which, notoriously, they are dazzled; and the orator who can sway them at his will, is more applauded than the successful general.

Such minds demand fervor, and even vehemence, in their speakers; and can, more easily, forgive a little infelicity of reasoning than tameness in sentiment or manner.

Among such people, most fortunately, HENRY CLAY found himself when the consciousness of his power, as an orator, first flashed upon him. In the town of his residence, many of the citizens were highly intelligent and refined; but "the country people," as they were termed,—those who constituted the mass of the population,—were distinguished by the characteristics of pioneer life; a resolute independence; thorough practical common sense; the utmost frankness of feeling and manners, and an unbounded admiration for rousing oratory.

A better field, for the development of young CLAY's peculiar eloquence, can not be imagined. By his early life, he had been taught better how to sympathize with, and to approach, his sturdy auditors, than he could have been by any instruction of the schools. His style of eloquence could not admit of being cramped. Its very success was dependent upon its hearty boldness. An audience of learned critics would have frozen the fountains of his inspiration. A careful regard to the nice structure of every sentence, and a perpetual dread lest, by some unlucky expression, he should offend "ears polite," would have effectually sealed the lips of one, like him, sensitively conscious of early disadvantages.

But the honest yeomanry and hardy hunters, who were to constitute the mass of his hearers, cared little about the nice balance of sentences, if so be those sentences conveyed sentiments which they could relish, in language which they could not mistake, and by tones and gestures which struck home to their hearts.

Occasions, likewise, favored the budding reputation of the

young orator. Demagogism was from the first abhorrent to his soul. However much he might seek to work upon the sympathies of his susceptible audiences, he never prostituted his powers to artifice, nor appealed to local and unworthy prejudices. He delighted in expatiating upon those cherished principles of freedom, for which our country had but just triumphantly fought. In such themes, he could indulge his loftiest declamation, without offense to his high sense of honor.

The promulgation of the "Alien and Sedition Laws," gave him his chosen opportunity. Those laws had their origin in a panic, which had seized upon many, lest our institutions should be overthrown by foreign emissaries, and the authority of our officers weakened, or destroyed, by the unbounded license of the press. They gave to the President authority to send into exile any person, whom he might deem dangerous to the well being of the Government, and guarded from assault, by special statute, the private and public character of those intrusted with responsible offices.

In endeavoring to correct, what was undoubtedly an evil, the Government was betrayed into an offense still more unpardonable. Freedom of personal movements and liberty of the press, are matters too sacred for governmental interference, except in cases of the most unusual and unquestionable necessity. The people considered their rights outraged. The disturbances of the Old World, the revolutionary proceedings of France, the turbulence of agents from abroad, the scurrility of the writers of pamphlets and newspapers, did not, in their opinion, constitute a necessity sufficient to warrant a scrutiny, like that of the Inquisition, and edicts which savored of despotism.

The laws met with vehement opposition. They could be popular in no part of a country, which was enjoying its first exultant consciousness of freedom. In Kentucky, they were especially odious. The habits of a pioneer people are abhorrent to every thing like constraint, whether in movements or in speech. They grow up in the enjoyment of almost unbounded license in respect to both. The people of Fayette called out their orators, to give utterance to their indignation.

After listening to the eloquence of one of their favorite and experienced leaders, with one accord and with great clamor, they shouted for Clay. Warm with the zeal of youth, ambitious for distinction, eager for the excitement of debate, unaffectedly indignant at the insult to freedom and to freemen, the young patriot responded to the call. To him the subject appeared, not in the light of an opportunity for successful demagogism, it was invested with the sacredness of liberty itself. The "inalienable rights," for which we had sent out a "declaration" to the world, and which, during eight years, we had defended at the point of the bayonet, were imperiled by our own rulers, upheld in their conduct by the deluded slaves of party zeal. The name Federalist, itself, was to himself and to many of his hearers an odious term. In the minds of not a few, it was associated with a tendency toward a concentration of power, ultimately a monarchy, and possibly a despotism.

Having such sentiments to work with, and such an audience to work upon, it is not wonderful that the enthusiastic eloquence of the youthful orator, roused the feelings of his hearers to almost a frenzy of excitement.

Those who were to follow in defense of the hated laws, except for the interposition of Clay, and the friend who had preceded him, would not have been permitted a hearing. As it was, they were suffered to proceed but a little way in their argument, before the people rushed upon them to hurl them down. With difficulty they were saved from personal indignity.

Among such a people, an orator like Clay could not fail of "a successful and lucrative practice." It is related of Erskine, that, after his first speech, he had placed in his hand retaining fees from thirty eminent lawyers. The services of Henry Clay, as we have abundant evidence, were considered at once equally desirable in every important suit.

His quickness to unravel the knotty points of a case, which had puzzled for a day or two the wits of his associate counsel, and his wonderful success in criminal causes, have come down to us with something, doubtless, of the exaggeration of tradition. Yet that his influence over a jury was, in no small degree, dangerous to the full attainment of justice, we may well believe, when we remember the fascination which, upon every subject, attended his eloquence.

It is related of him with much enthusiasm, that, at a trial for capital offense, in Harrison county, in which two Germans, father and son, stood indicted for a brutal murder, he succeeded, first, in obtaining a verdict of homicide, and afterward, an arrest of judgment, resulting in their acquittal.

In another instance, though the evidence seemed demonstrative against his client, he prevailed so far as to divide the jury; and, upon a second trial, to procure a discharge, by setting up the remarkable plea, that no man could have his life twice imperiled for the same offense, and that, to continue the prosecution, would constitute such a case.

To carry his point, he found it necessary to back his plea by such a trial of his personal consequence, as never could succeed except where great popularity had given occasion for the utmost self-confidence; demurring at the objections of the court, to his peculiar construction of the case, and gathering up his documents, he was about to leave the court-room. The *ruse*,—for such we must consider it,—succeeded, and he was urged to come back and conduct the trial in his own way. The result, as we might expect, was the discharge of the prisoner.

Such instances, whatever value they may or may not have, in establishing HENRY CLAY's character with the reader, as an accurate and thorough lawyer, certainly prove that his eloquence was of a very effective order, and that his personal influence, thus early, was almost unbounded.

While prosperity was thus attending HENRY CLAY in his public career, he was adding to his private happiness, by bringing around himself the comforts of a home. With social affections keenly active, he early sought that high sympathy and companionship which can be found only in marriage.

In April, 1799, when he was but twenty-two years of age, he was united in marriage to Lucretia Hart, the daughter of Col. Hart, one of the most influential and hospitable citizens of Lexington. Two years afterward we find him, in a letter to Judge

Brooke of Virginia, speaking of his home, with a settled gravity and that peculiar air of consequence, which seem especially to befit the father of a family. We can not forbear giving an extract from this letter, since it not only indicates the feeling we have described, but also the high-toned generosity of his character, and the eagerness with which, at the earliest opportunity, he offers a return for past favors.

After speaking of some business matters, he adds: "What has become of the son of my much regretted friend, your brother? I feel myself under obligations of gratitude to the father, which I should be happy of having an opportunity of discharging to the son. What is the progress he has made in his education? We have, in this place, a university in a very flourishing condition. Could you not spare him to me, in this country, for two or three years? I live at a short distance from the buildings, have a small family, and need not add that, from the cheapness of living in this country, his expense to me would be extremely inconsiderable. We have, too, a distant hope of getting Mr. Madison, from 'William and Mary,' to take the management of our seminary. Be pleased to let me hear from you on this subject."

For domestic life, we may believe, judging from his temperament, he had a keen relish. But of domestic life he was not destined to partake largely. His talents forbade his living, in any exclusive sense, to himself. He was needed by his country. Before it had been possible for him to build up any great or lasting character as a lawyer, he was called to enter upon what became the special business of his life,—the toils of statesmanship. Without any solicitation of his own, and while he was absent among the mountains for his health, his name was brought forward in connection with a seat in the State Legislature. His competitors were popular; he started late in the canvass, but his personal presence at the critical juncture,—his remarkable tact, as displayed in his quick reply to the hunters, when, without any practice in rifle-shooting, he claimed to be an excellent shot, and, favored by chance, won the hearts of the rude backwoodsmen by planting the bullet in the center of the mark,—and, most of all, the fascination of his eloquence overcame all obstacles, and insured for him a complete triumph. His first legislative exploits pertained to matters of local interest, and were conducted with much sparring and direct personal encounter; a mode of debate sure to elicit the applause of a rude and popularly constituted assembly.

The contest between himself and a member of the name of Grundy, constituted the principal interest of his first session. It was doubtless that kind of intellectual gladiatorship, which young and ambitious minds delight in when they first awake to the consciousness of considerable power; confident and impetuous, they are ready to measure swords with every opponent, and covet the admiration of the multitude who cheer them on.

But CLAY soon vindicated his supremacy, and feeling himself *facile princeps*, was, thenceforward, better situated to advance business and devise measures for the true welfare of the State. For, until a man's position is established, his attention will be absorbed by his own claims, and his views will likewise lack the weight which comes from confirmed personal influence.

The degree of self-confidence and personal consideration, to which he soon attained, as well as the peculiar class of minds with which he had to deal, may be seen in the effect which a few jocular remarks from him produced, when it was proposed to remove the seat of government. CLAY was in favor of the removal, and in ridicule of the peculiar position of Frankfort, which is in a deep valley, surrounded by abrupt hills, compared it first to an inverted hat, and afterward changing the figure, called it nature's penitentiary, pointing to a ragged and now scampering group in the galleries, as a specimen of the prisoners. The witticism proved as effective as a logical argument; the point was carried, and Frankfort, if any other place could have been agreed upon, would have ceased to be the capital. It is right to say that CLAY, some years afterward, made honorable amends by apologizing for this injustice to a very beautiful town.

The nobleness of his character and his dauntless manner, at this time, are illustrated by his espousing the cause of a humble innkeeper, who could find no one else willing to undertake it, against the United States Attorney, Daviess, from whom he had received insolent treatment, and so warmly as to receive at a pause in the trial, a note of intimidation, but which Clay persisted in disregarding so far as to provoke from the offended attorney a challenge. The duel was prevented, however, by the interposition of friends.

Having once set out in the career of politics, there was to be for Clay no turning back. General Adair of Kentucky, resigned his seat in the United States Senate, and Clay, though but twenty-nine years of age, was selected to fill the vacancy. As he was about setting out on his journey to Washington, he received the following letter from Aaron Burr:

"Dear Sir—Information has this morning been given me, that Mr. Daviess has recommenced his prosecution and inquiry. I must entreat your professional aid in this business. It would be disagreeable to me to form a new connection, and various considerations will, it is hoped, induce you, even at some personal inconvenience, to acquiesce in my request. I shall, however, insist on making a liberal pecuniary compensation. The delay of your journey to Washington, for a few days, can not be very material. No business is done in Congress until after new year. I pray you to repair to Frankfort on receipt of this."

Public opinion was at this time greatly divided, as to Burr's innocence of any treasonable intentions. By many the prosecution against him was regarded as the offspring of party malice. Burr, himself, was careful to remove any scruples which busy rumor might have created in the mind of Clay. He addressed him a second note, in which he pleads innocence in the following unqualified terms:

"Sir—I have no design, nor have I taken any measure, to promote a dissolution of the Union, or a separation of any one or more States from the residue. I have neither published a line on the subject, nor has any one through my agency or with my knowledge. I have no design to intermeddle with the Government, or to disturb the tranquillity of the United States, or of its Territories, or any part of them. I have neither issued, nor signed, nor promised a commission to any person, for any purpose. I do not own a musket, nor a bayonet, nor any single article of military stores, nor does any person for me, by my authority, or with my knowledge.

"My views have been fully explained to, and approved by, several of the principal officers of Government, and, I believe, are well understood by the administration, and seen by it with complacency. They are such as every man of honor, and every good citizen, must approve.

"Considering the high station you now fill in our national councils, I have thought these explanations proper, as well to counteract the chimerical tales, which malevolent persons have so industriously circulated, as to satisfy you that you have not espoused the cause of a man unfriendly to the laws, the Government, or the interests of his country."

Clay was deceived by the apparent candor of Burr, and the heartiness of his disavowal. So pressing an application to a young lawyer, from one who had filled a highly distinguished place in the regards of his country, could not have been otherwise than flattering. He undertook the defense, but as the grand jury returned the indictment, accompanied with a refusal to consider it a true bill, he was absolved from any active part in the matter. Upon repairing to Washington he was shown evidence, which satisfied him, of the criminal intentions of Burr.

The endeavor was made to fasten odium upon Clay, because of the part which he had assumed. In this attempt party malignity to some extent succeeded; but to us, who, at a distance, can look impartially upon the occurrences of that day, the eager endeavor of Burr to establish his innocence in the eyes of the young Senator, is all the vindication of his own integrity, which Clay could wish.

We follow Clay now to his seat in the Senate of the United States. It is not to be supposed that, occupying it for but one session, and feeling conscious of being one of the youngest members, he took a remarkably active part in the deliberations of that body. He found occasion, however, to advocate various plans for internal improvement.

His maiden speech was upon the construction of a bridge over the Potomac; a matter of local interest, but involving a question of constitutional power. He brought to the subject the results of extensive investigation, and his speech upon the occasion was esteemed equal to the fame which had preceded him.

His efforts were likewise directed to the construction of a canal in his own State, and improvements in the navigation of the Ohio River,—harbingers of the policy to which he was afterward committed, and by which no small degree of his great subsequent popularity was secured.

Upon returning to his friends, he was again elected to a seat in the State Legislature, and was made Speaker of its lower House. That he filled this office with dignity, it can not be necessary to assert, while his signal ability in a still higher station of the same character, is still a matter of memory.

In 1808, his friends, from a desire to match him against his principal political opponent, Humphrey Marshall, saw fit not to re-elect him Speaker. The debates assumed an acrimonious turn. Some offensive remarks, by Marshall, upon a resolution introduced by CLAY, to the effect that all the members should, for the sake of encouraging home industry, clothe themselves in garments of domestic manufacture, called forth a challenge from the latter. The parties met, exchanged two or three shots, were both slightly wounded, when, by the interference of their seconds, they were prevented from pursuing any further their murderous diversion.

One effort of HENRY CLAY, during his last connection with the State Legislature, deserves to be recorded forever to his credit. It was his valiant and successful opposition, almost single-handed, to a measure which prejudice and demagogism would have carried through, to the everlasting discredit of Kentucky. An unqualified hatred to England led to the strange proposal, that the decisions of her courts should never be cited as precedents, nor allowed any weight at any Kentucky bar. Illiberality could not well go further. Yet so great was the unenlightened zeal of the Legislature, that its purpose was defeated only by the most strenuous efforts of Clay, exerted through personal influence, through argument, and through the seductive power of his eloquence.

Henry Clay's career, in the limited sphere of a State Legislature, we are now to see draw to a close. His talents are for wider fields and loftier displays. The skill which he has acquired, is to be transferred permanently to that arena where he can accomplish most for his country and for his race. But while we dismiss him from his narrower stage, we must show, from the testimony of one who knew how he there acquitted himself, that his success was not the result of accident; that by no "chance hits," and by no fitful efforts in these earlier years of discipline, was laid the foundation of the brilliant, useful, and enduring structure of his future fame.

"He appears," says the writer alluded to, "to have been the pervading spirit of the whole body. He never came to the debates without the knowledge necessary to the perfect elucidation of his subject, and he always had the power of making his knowledge so practical, and lighting it up so brightly with the fire of eloquence, and the living soul of intellect, that, without resorting to the arts of insidiousness, he could generally control the movements of the Legislature at will. His was not an undue influence; it was the simple ascendency of mind over mind. The bills, which originated with him, instead of being characterized by the eccentricities and ambitious innovations which are too often visible in the course of young men of genius, suddenly elevated to power and influence, were remarkable only for their plain common sense, and their tendency to advance the general interests of the State. Though he carried his plans into effect by the aid of the magical incantations of the orator, he always conceived them with the coolness and discretion of a philosopher. No subject was so great as to baffle his powers,—none so minute as to elude them. He could handle the telescope and the microscope with equal skill. In him, the haughty demagogues of the Legislature found an antagonist, who never failed to foil them in their bold projects, and the intriguers of lower degree were baffled with equal certainty, whenever they attempted to get any petty measure through the House for their own personal gratification, or that of their friends. The people, therefore, justly regarded him as emphatically their own."

CHAPTER IV.

Senate of the United States again—Policy of our country—Mr. Clay advocates protection of domestic manufactures—Opposes a United States Bank—His activity in bringing about a war with England—Declaration of war.

Mr. Clay entered the Senate of the United States a second time, in the winter of 1809–10. So short had been the political history of our country, that no great systems, either of foreign or of domestic policy, had been established. The wants and capabilities of the country were hardly known. The course of legislation had been rather a series of experiments than any thing stable and definite. The political character of the nation was undergoing a formative process. The problem, whether Federal or Democratic principles should obtain the predominance, was hastening to a solution. Upon the result of this important question, hung suspended the future distinctive policy of the nation.

That problem, to all intents and purposes, was solved by the administration of Jefferson. The Democratic element then gained a predominance, which, except in a few fluctuations, it has ever since retained. Yet, while the prevailing spirit of the country may be characterized as the eager, restless, aggressive spirit of a Democracy, it is not of such a Democracy as floated before the vision of the early champions of State rights.

Federalism has not been annihilated, but absorbed. The country to-day, while it is more intensely democratic than it was fifty years ago, is also ruled more upon federal principles. While every year makes us a fiercer Democracy, every year also consolidates the power of the Central Government. Except in the instance of one or two States, the feeling of State pride is merging more and more into patriotic pride for the Union. Sectional causes, indeed, disturb the surface of this feeling and check its growth; yet the evidence that it exists may be found in any casual newspaper, published in any part of the country. Where one paragraph is given,—always excepting the newspapers of South Carolina,—to the glorification of the State, ten paragraphs may be found of exultant pride, which, in case of threatened war, rises into bravado, in the extent, the resources, the power of "The Great American people."

The country has, in fact, become a consolidated Democracy. This direction of its development, as we have intimated, was effected largely by the influence of Jefferson. Its career in that direction was but just inaugurated when CLAY, in 1810, a second time entered the Senate.

The country was ready, and waiting for the minds which were to mark out and fix its subsequent policy. Of those minds CLAY'S was eminently one. At the very outset, not as though yet he saw the way clearly, but rather as though he beheld "men as trees walking," he advocated what afterward grew into the American Protective System.

The immediate occasion of his first argument upon the subject was a bill, to the effect that, in procuring cordage, sail-cloths and ordinary munitions of war, preference, if possible, should be given to articles of domestic manufacture. His views in the immediate instance were acted upon, and a most favorable impulse, especially considering the necessity for home industry which the war quickly following entailed, was given to the manufacturing interests of the country.

The interest of this, his first reported speech, is greatly hightened by the fact, that the policy therein advocated was a favorite one with him through life; one to which he devoted the most study; upon which he expended the most ingenuity, and battled for with the most persistency.

His arguments, except in comprehensiveness, were similar to those which he afterward adduced when the special champion of that policy; arguments which will always have different degrees of weight, according to the side which individuals espouse of that much disputed question, the propriety of a protective tariff.

In the winter session of 1810-11, the Senate was called upon to decide the question whether the charter of the United States Bank should be renewed. The Bank was incorporated in 1791, and its charter would expire by limitation, in 1811.

Mr. Clay believed, with the mass of the Republican party, that the Constitution made no provision for granting such a charter. The Legislature of his State had also laid him under instructions to oppose it. He therefore assailed the Bank with all his power of logic, and all the keenness of his sarcasm. He directed his blows, especially, against what he supposed its weakest side,—its lack of constitutional warrant.

As the United States Bank became afterward a favorite measure with him, his change of views gave occasion to his opponents to charge him with gross inconsistency. But pitiable, indeed, would be the lot of erring humanity, if a man must retain unchanged to his dying hour, the opinions which he may have embraced in the immaturity, and with the haste of youth. The highest definition of consistency is not that which limits it to perseverance in a given course, under all circumstances, and against every degree of conviction to the contrary. In such a quality, Clay might feel no shame to plead deficient.

But if the question should be in regard to consistency, even in its general acceptation,—namely, an undeviating pursuit of the same specific ends,—political history, we are confident, can present few more striking instances of it than Clay's. In old age he was seen fighting still under the same banner which he himself had raised in the exultant strength of his youth. His last efforts were in behalf of a domestic policy and the integrity of the Union, and so likewise were his first. The sturdy Democratic principles with which he set out in his political career, he retained through life,—holding them, not alone during the sunshine of popular favor, but battling for them in darkness and in trial, against the opposition of iron-willed enemies, and the treachery of false friends.

He himself referred to this single change of views many years afterward, when there could have been no occasion for insincerity, in the following words:

"I never, but once, changed my opinion on any great measure of national policy, or any great principle of construction of the National Constitution. In early life, on deliberate consideration, I adopted the principles of interpreting the Federal Constitution, which had been so ably developed and enforced by Mr. Madison, in his memorable report to the Virginia Legislature, and to them, as I understood them, I have constantly adhered. Upon the question coming up in the Senate of the United States, to re-charter the first Bank of the United States, thirty years ago, I opposed the re-charter, upon convictions which I honestly entertained. The experience of the war which shortly followed, the condition into which the currency of the country was thrown without a bank, and, I may now add, later and more disastrous experience, convinced me I was wrong. I publicly stated to my constituents, in a speech in Lexington (that which I made in the House of Representatives of the United States not having been reported), my reasons for that change, and they are preserved in the archives of the country. I appeal to that record; and I am willing to be judged, now and hereafter, by their validity."

Mr. CLAY's term in the Senate, which was but for two years, having ended in 1811, he returned to his home at Lexington. But Kentucky could not dispense with services so fitted for public life and legislation. He was immediately elected to a seat in the House of Representatives,—and so conspicuous had he already become by his talents, and so great was his popularity, that, upon the first ballot at the opening of the session, he was made Speaker of that body,—an honor never accorded before to one whose person was a stranger in its halls, and whose voice was untried in its debates.

A proud moment must that have been to the young Kentucky Congressman, when his merit, owing nothing to birth, nothing to early advantages, and but little to outward circumstances of any kind, was at once recognized with homage, by those who could boast of all; and when the applause, which greeted the announcement of his election, revealed the strong force of enthusiastic friends who would rally, at any time, to his support, as they had now rallied to render his entrance among them a triumph.

He might appreciate the more highly the compliment, because the session promised to be a most important and stirring one. Europe was in arms, and the convulsion of one continent threatened to shake the stability of the other. War was teaching that lesson which it inculcates more emphatically than any other mentor,—the mutual dependence of the different families of the human race; that one member can not suffer without all the other members suffering with it.

The Berlin and Milan decrees of Napoleon, and the orders in Council of England, had subjected our commerce to most ruinous restrictions. All the important ports of Europe were declared in a state of blockade. Our trading vessels were constantly exposed to confiscation. The only choice left to our merchants was to permit their ships to rot idly at their wharves, or to engage them in commerce by stealth, and at the imminent risk of seizure.

Troubles had been deepening, too, for years. Our young country was regarded by England with hatred and contempt. Her officers, in foreign service, omitted no opportunity of displaying toward us their insolence. One of our own vessels of war, without just provocation, had been fired into, almost within our own waters.

No indignity, however, excited such universal anger as the course of British officers, in forcibly entering our ships, and, under the pretext of searching for their fugitive sailors, impressing our seamen. According to a statement in Congress, seven thousand of our countrymen were, at the moment of the report, forcibly detained in her service.

All remonstrance proved ineffectual. Lord Castlereagh treated contemptuously the idea that England would relinquish her right of search. To Mr. Russel, our *Charge d'Affaires*, to whom was intrusted a negotiation with the British Government, he stated, in language which he desired not to be mistaken:

"There has evidently been much misapprehension on this subject; an erroneous belief entertained, that an arrangement in regard to it has been nearer an accomplishment than the facts will warrant. Even our friends in Congress,—I mean those who are opposed to going to war with us,—have been so confident in this mistake, that they have ascribed the failure of such an arrangement solely to the misconduct of the American Government. This error probably originated with Mr. King, for, being much esteemed here, and always well received by persons in power, he seems to have misconstrued their readiness to listen to his representations, and their warm professions of a disposition to remove the complaints of America in relation to impressment, into a supposed conviction, on their part, of the propriety of adopting the plan which he had proposed."

There was, therefore, throughout the country, an indignant cry for war. In Congress the belligerent spirit was predominant. Still, the party in opposition was far enough from being insignificant. Nearly all the Federalists were opposed to a rupture with England. Of the State Rights party, Randolph, one of the ablest, exerted his influence, sometimes by logic, sometimes by rhetoric, and sometimes by ridicule, unceasingly against it. In his eyes, a war with England was an alliance with Napoleon, whom, from his rapacious spirit of conquest, he designated "the arch enemy of mankind." The capture of Canada, one of the professed objects of the war, he sneered at as preposterous. He deprecated the fostering of a military and aggressive spirit, which the existence of an army and a navy would be sure to promote.

The session was, therefore, a stormy one. The country did not ride into war with all sails set and colors flying, and by the breath of only prospering gales. Notwithstanding the prevalent hatred to England, and the war sentiment predominant in Congress, it required the logic of Calhoun, and the martial enthusiasm of CLAY, to nerve their fellow-members into a warlike attitude.

In the President's message of November 4, 1811, the causes of complaint against England were reviewed. The message was referred to a committee, of which Peter B. Porter of New York, was chairman. The resolutions which they reported were unmistakably warlike. Still, as the formation of committees was under the control of the Speaker, those resolutions could be regarded as expressing the sentiments of only a party.

The Senate transmitted to the House, on the thirty-first of December, a bill providing for the raising of twenty-five thousand troops. CLAY, leaving the chair, made it the occasion for a most enthusiastic speech in favor of war. He had committed himself to that policy, and it was never his characteristic to do things by halves. High spirited and impetuous, he could no more brook an insult to his country than to himself. He viewed the aspect of affairs with the partiality of the advocate, rather than with the wily coolness of the diplomatist. He was desirous to precipitate matters. What he did, he would do boldly. Since he had given his voice for war, he would have every preparation made to constitute it a successful war. In this he proved himself worthy to be a leader. A large class of men, after deciding upon a course of conduct,—such a course, even, as from its very nature demands promptness and intrepidity,—display a miserable infirmity of will, and signally fail, because what they desire they have not the courage to perform.

It was not so with CLAY. Whatever his judgment or his feelings dictated, his will shrank not from executing. A part of those who were committed in favor of war, trembled at the prospect of so large a standing army as twenty-five thousand men. To order such a levy, they seemed to feel, was to pledge themselves to all the unknown horrors of war. That such was its bearing and intention, CLAY unhesitatingly avowed. He justly contended, that it was "too great for peace, but," as he feared, "too small for war." If his country was to engage with England, he would have it enter the contest equipped, not for defeat, but for victory.

On the twenty-second of January, a report was made, by a committee to whom the matter had been intrusted, in favor of increasing the navy. To this, also, CLAY gave his earnest support. His plan contemplated not what was extravagant and

4

impracticable. He deluded not himself nor the House with the idea that a naval force might be created, able to cope in numbers with the proud marine of England. But he demanded that such additions should be made as might effectually protect our coasting trade, and our many ports, from the insolence of every passing cruiser. The Navy bill, like that of the Army Appropriation, was adopted by a large majority. This was upon the twenty-ninth of January, 1812.

Upon the first day of April, the President sent a secret message to Congress, recommending an embargo for sixty days. This was acknowledged by the war party to be preparatory to an appeal to arms.

Mr. Randolph rose, and, with much solemnity, exclaimed: "I am so impressed with the importance of the subject, and the solemnity of the occasion, that I can not be silent. Sir, we are now in conclave; the eyes of the surrounding world are not upon us; we are shut up here from the light of heaven, but the eyes of God are upon us. He knows the spirit of our minds. Shall we deliberate upon this subject with the spirit of sobriety and candor, or with that spirit which has too often characterized our discussions upon occasions like the present? We ought to realize that we are in the presence of that God who knows our thoughts and motives, and to whom we must hereafter render an account for the deeds done in the body. I hope, sir, the spirit of party, and every improper passion, will be exorcised; that our hearts may be as pure and clean as falls to the lot of human nature.

"I will appeal to the sobriety and reflection of the House, and ask what *new* cause of war for the last twelve months? What new cause of embargo within that period? The affair of Chesapeake is settled,—no new principle interpolated into the laws of nations. I suppose every man of candor and sober reflection will ask, why we did not go to war twelve months ago? Or, will it be said we ought to make up by our promptness now, for our slowness then? It is not generally wise to dive into futurity, but it is wise to profit by experience, although it may be unpleasant. I feel much concerned to have the bill on the table for one hour."

The Federal party, through some of their representatives, assumed a tone still more deprecatory. Josiah Quincey of Massachusetts, openly avowed that he had sent dispatches to eastern merchants, that their vessels might leave port before the embargo should take effect. "We did it," he said, "to escape into the jaws of the British Lion and of the French Tiger, which are places of repose, of joy, and delight, when compared with the grasp and fang of this hyena embargo. Look now upon the river below Alexandria, and you will see the sailors towing down their vessels, as from a pestilence, against wind and tide, anxious to escape from a country which would destroy instead of preserving them. I object to it, because it is no efficient preparation; because it is not a progress toward honorable war, but a subterfuge from the question. If we must perish, let us perish by any hand except our own."

From these extracts it can be seen that the opposition was wanting neither in strength nor clamor. CLAY rested uneasily in his seat as Speaker, under such arguments and appeals. His spirit longed to be in the thickest of the fight. Yielding the chair to others, he often descended to the floor of the House to confront audacity with equal boldness—and to answer the question, "What cause is there for war?" by depicting the commerce of his country ruined, her honor insulted, her name a byword and term of derision abroad.

Randolph had said, in the course of the speech from which we have quoted, "I am confident in the declaration, Mr. Chairman, that this (the embargo) is not a measure of the Executive; but that it is engendered by an extensive excitement upon the Executive."

Madison, indeed, seems to have labored under an infirmity of purpose. Although he had committed himself so far as to lay the embargo, it was not until he had been waited upon by CLAY in an informal deputation, and had caught the contagion of his enthusiasm, that he submitted the message to Congress which was to result in an appeal to arms. Both Houses of Congress took decisive action upon the subject on the eighteenth of June, and on the nineteenth, by proclamation of the President, war existed between the United States and England.

CHAPTER V.

Early disasters of the war—Subsequent successes—Negotiations for peace—Ghent—Mr. CLAY a Commissioner—Terms of the treaty—Mr. CLAY visits England—United States Bank—Mr. CLAY's change of views—What constitutes true Political Economy—Compensation bill—CLAY is obliged to canvass his State—South American independence.

THE credit or the blame of the second war with England, whichever it be, must unquestionably fall mainly to the share of CLAY. For an appeal to arms he had battled with the ardor of a patriot, and with a vehemence inspired by opposition.

The war opened disastrously. General Hull surrendered his army at Detroit. A series of similar reverses followed in its train. The depression occasioned by such calamities is vividly conveyed in the following letter from General Harrison to Mr. CLAY:

"I write to you, my dear sir, amid a thousand interruptions; and I do it solely for the purpose of showing you, that you are present to my recollection, under circumstances that would almost justify a suspension of every private feeling. The rumored disasters upon our northwestern frontier, are now ascertained to be correct. The important point of Mackinac was surrendered without an effort; an army captured at Detroit, after receiving three shots from a *distant* battery of the enemy (and from the range of which it was easy to retire), a fort [Chicago], in the midst of hostile tribes of Indians, ordered to be evacuated, and the garrison slaughtered; the numerous northwestern tribes of Indians (with the exception of two feeble ones), in arms against us, is the distressing picture which presents itself to view in this part of the country.

"To remedy all these misfortunes, I have an army competent in numbers, and in spirit equal to any that Greece or Rome ever boasted of, but destitute of artillery, of many necessary equipments, and absolutely ignorant of every military evolution; nor have I but a single individual capable of assisting me in training them."

This gloomy state of affairs, however, soon passed away. England, exultant, especially upon her own chosen element, the sea, was made to lower her tone of insolent superiority. The Constitution encountered the Guerriere, and captured it, after a short, most decisive and brilliant engagement. An English statesman was constrained to declare upon the floor of Parliament, that the spell of invincibility, in which their marine had gloried, was effectually broken.

Upon the lakes, America gained renewed laurels. The spirit of the people rose with the return of the tide of success. Washington, to the mortification of the country, was taken and sacked, but upon the north-western frontier, Scott was retrieving the fortunes of his Government, and vindicating the bravery of its people.

Meanwhile, Russia offered her interposition to bring about peace. The United States accepted her offer, but England expressed a preference for a negotiation between commissioners, appointed severally by the belligerent parties.

As Clay had been the principal instigator of war, so he was selected as one of the negotiators of peace. It was proposed at first to meet at Gottingen, but, by agreement of the commissioners, Ghent was afterward selected. Albert Gallatin, James A. Bayard, John Q. Adams and Jonathan Russel acted, with Mr. Clay, for the American Government; Lord Gambier, Henry Goulborne and William Adamos, for the British.

The English commissioners were able, from their nearness to home, to refer every important matter to the consideration of the power which had appointed them. The dispatches of the American commissioners to their Government were, unexpectedly to themselves, spread before the people. It was feared that this ill-advised proceeding would embarrass negotiations. Lord Gambier, when the subject was alluded to in his presence by Mr. CLAY, purposely to call out his opinion, expressed his unqualified surprise at an action so entirely without precedent in diplomatic experience. Mr. CLAY gave the subject a most ingenious and characteristic turn. He represented to Lord Gambier, that to lay the matter thus before the people was equivalent only to what the British commissioners had done, in referring matters to their home Government; for that, in the United States, the whole American people were the repositories of power, and that directly to them the commissioners stood responsible.

After long discussion in regard to the Fisheries, the right to which the English wished to recall; the navigation of the Mississippi, which they demanded for their vessels, upon equal terms with ours; the right of protection over the Indians, which they claimed, and a boundary line which would deprive us of a large portion of our territory, but which they ceased to contend for, the terms of peace were agreed upon. American rights were established upon a footing which they had never before enjoyed. The commerce of the ocean was released from its intolerable restrictions. The odious right of search was relinquished. The navigation of the Mississippi was denied to English vessels. The privilege of fishing in British waters was not withdrawn. The impertinent claim to extend a supervision over our Indian tribes, was abandoned. And so well were the principal rights which were contended for established, that America never since has had occasion for those complaints which drove her reluctantly into conflict with her haughty foe. This fact HENRY CLAY might proudly point to, in vindication of the earnestness with which he pleaded for a war in defense of "Free Trade and Sailors' Rights." What he had urged his country to contend for, upon sea and upon land, at the cannon's mouth, he labored effectually to secure in the peaceable encounters of diplomacy. Having proved himself zealous for his country's rights in her halls of legislation, he proved, also, that he might be trusted to demand for her abroad, all that justice might claim, or that a foe, whose insolence was somewhat subdued, might be expected to yield.

After concluding negotiations, Mr. CLAY proceeded to Paris. He delayed, as yet, to go to England; for during his residence at Ghent, he had heard with chagrin of the capture of Washington. But while he remained undecided, the intelligence came of the battle of New Orleans. "Now," he exclaimed, "I can go to England without mortification."

In England, Mr. CLAY received not only every attention which his official character would naturally elicit, but the most flattering regard from men who would not have bestowed it except where they had discovered agreeable qualities, and been affected with sincere admiration. Sir James Mackintosh, of whom Mr. Macaulay says: "His mind was a vast magazine, admirably arranged; every thing was there, and every thing was in its place. His judgments on men, on sects, on books, had been often and carefully tested and weighed, and had then been committed each to its proper receptacle, in the most capacious and accurately constructed memory that any human being ever possessed. It would have been strange, indeed, if you had asked for any thing that was not to be found in that immense storehouse;"—Sir James Mackintosh wrote to the youthful American diplomatist the following flattering note:

"Sir James Mackintosh is so eager to have the honor of Mr. CLAY's acquaintance, that he ventures to request his company this evening to a small party, when Lady Mackintosh will be most happy to receive him, at nine or ten o'clock, with any gentleman of his suit who may be so good as to honor them with coming."

In September, 1815, Mr. CLAY returned to his own country, and shortly afterward entered Congress, to which he had been re-elected during his absence. He was chosen Speaker a second time. As the procuring cause of the war, and the negotiator of the subsequent peace, he felt called upon to stand forth as the champion of the treaty, against its opposers.

"Whatever diversity of opinion," he said, "may have existed as to the declaration of the war, there are some points on which all may look back with proud satisfaction. The first relates to the time of the conclusion of the peace. Had it been immediately after the treaty of Paris, we should have retired humiliated from the contest, believing that we had escaped the severe chastisement with which we were threatened; and that we owed to the generosity and magnanimity of the enemy, what we were incapable of commanding by our arms. That magnanimity would have been the theme of every tongue, and of every press, abroad and at home. We should have retired, unconscious of our strength, and unconscious of the utter inability of the enemy, with his whole undivided force, to make any serious impressions upon us. Our military character, then in the lowest state of degradation, would have been unretrieved.

"Fortunately for us, Great Britain chose to try the issue of the last campaign. And the issue of the last campaign has demonstrated, in the repulse before Baltimore, the retreat from Plattsburg, the hard-fought action on the Niagara frontier, and in that most glorious day, the eighth of January, that we have always possessed the finest elements of military composition; and that a proper use of them, only, was necessary to insure, for the army and militia, a fame as imperishable as that which the navy had previously acquired.

"Another point, which appears to me to afford the highest consolation is, that we fought the most powerful nation perhaps in existence, single-handed and alone, without any sort of alliance. More than thirty years has Great Britain been maturing her physical means, which she had rendered as efficacious as possible, by skill, by discipline, and by actual service. Proudly boasting of the conquest of Europe, she vainly flattered herself with the easy conquest of America, also. Her veterans were put to flight, or defeated, while all Europe,—I mean the governments of Europe,—was gazing, with cold indifference or sentiments of positive hatred of us, upon the arduous contest. Hereafter, no monarch can assert claims of gratitude upon us for assistance rendered in the hour of danger.

"There is another view of which the subject of the war is fairly susceptible. From the moment that Great Britain came forward at Ghent with her extravagant demands, the war totally changed in character. It became, as it were, a new war. It was no longer an American war, prosecuted for objects of British aggressions upon American rights, but became a British war, prosecuted for objects of British ambition, to be accompanied by American sacrifices. And what were those demands? They consisted of the erection of a barrier between Canada and the United States, to be formed by cutting off from Ohio and some of the Territories, a country more extensive than Great Britain, containing thousands of freemen, who were to be abandoned to their fate, and creating a new power totally unknown upon the continent of America; of the dismantling of our fortresses and naval power on the lakes, with the surrender of the military occupation of those waters to the enemy; and of an *arrondissement* for two British provinces. These demands, boldly asserted, and one of them declared to be a *sine qua non*, were finally relinquished. Taking this view of the subject, if there be loss of reputation by either party, in the terms of peace, who has sustained it?

"The effects of the war are highly satisfactory. Abroad, our character, which at the time of its declaration was in the lowest state of degradation, is raised to the highest point of elevation. It is impossible for any American to visit Europe without being sensible of this agreeable change, in the personal attentions which he receives, in the praises which are bestowed on our past exertions, and the predictions which are made as to our future prospects."

In the winter session of 1815–16, President Madison recommended the establishment of a National Bank, as a measure of relief for the financial embarrassments of the country. On the eighth of January, 1816, John C. Calhoun, chairman of the committee to which the subject had been referred, reported in favor of the institution. CLAY, in the noble ingenuousness of his nature, did not fear to come out, despite his former views, and give the whole weight of his influence in favor of the measure. He knew that he rendered himself liable to the charge of fickleness and inconsistency. He knew that the bloodhounds of party would follow upon the trail and raise a clamor at his expense. But, whether right or wrong in his views, he had become convinced that, for the financial distresses of the country, there was no other remedy. He hesitated not, therefore, to sacrifice the appearance of consistency to the supposed welfare of his country. He advocated the measure in Congress, until he saw it brought to a successful issue, and justified his course, with the utmost appearance of candor, to his constituents at home. That he was sincere in his change of views, we can have no just occasion to doubt.

The country, at the close of the war, felt the effects of that sudden revulsion which always attends a sudden change from hostilities to peace. Manufactures which, during the suspension of commerce, flourished without competition, languished when peace whitened again the sea with sails. Domestic labor could not stand before the foreign competition. Our people would not submit to work for prices which the half famished artisans of the Manchesters and Birminghams of England were glad to accept.

War, too, creates special branches of business, and furnishes employment in ways peculiar to itself. The restoration of peace is, therefore, the discharge of thousands from situations, upon the continuance of which, depended their daily bread.

In addition to all this, a sudden and oppressive debt hangs like an incubus upon the energies of a nation, at the moment it leaves the toils of war to resume the kindlier arts of peace.

At such emergencies, the people look expectantly to their legislators. They have not the political sagacity which would enable them to wait in confident hope, for time to bring the wished-for changes; and even if they possessed the sagacity, they would hardly exercise the patience. Like one laboring under a painful disease, the agony of which, nevertheless, is the outworking of the malady and the salvation of the patient, they demand an instant remedy, not reflecting that a temporary suppression of pain may prove, in the end, disastrous and fatal.

The physician and the legislator feel also, each in their separate departments, that since it is their province to relieve suffering and restore to health, they will be wanting in their duty, unless, by some heroic remedy, they remove the visible, undeniable evidences of distress. So that, looking more to present relief than to permanent benefit; yielding themselves rather to the impulse of their feelings than to the calm conviction of their judgments, they often institute measures, in all sincerity, which afterward none would regret more than themselves.

The United States Bank, we conceive to have been such a measure; yet, at the same time, we believe that CLAY, and Calhoun, and Madison, and the host of others who approved of it, acted under the firmest conviction, that thus they were best promoting the interests of their country, and meriting the approval of patriots. Nor need we wonder that this should be so, for political science, though capable of being reduced to rigid rules and to a simple system, is yet but one of the youngest of the sciences; and it labors, moreover, under the disadvantage that disorders in the body politic can often be corrected only by years of patient waiting, extending, not unfrequently, beyond the lives of the existing generation. But, as we have indicated, it is not in the nature of man to wait so long in hope. Something must be done at once, and if the regular physician, if the true legislator will not do it, resort will be had to some medical or political quack, according as the case may be, who will promise most largely, and administer his remedies most heroically. It is difficult, also, when not enlightened by experience, to keep accurately in the mind relations of cause and effect, which are separated by so wide an interval.

If we are wiser to-day than the statesmen of forty years ago, it is not because we have clearer heads, or sounder judgments, or larger patriotism, but because the science of legislation has advanced, and that, too, by their very instrumentality; because they, by going over the ground before us, have guarded us from error, by even their very blunders, and have bequeathed to us the accumulated treasures of their experience.

Soon after the passage of the bill establishing the United States Bank, Mr. Clay made himself somewhat unpopular by voting for what was called the Compensation bill. The pay of members of Congress had been six dollars *per diem*. A bill was introduced to substitute a salary of fifteen hundred dollars for the session, in place of the *per diem* allowance.

Clay found it necessary to canvass his own State, in opposition to his former colleague, to secure his seat. His popularity was, however, proof against even this undemocratic measure, as it was thought, and he was returned again to Congress. At the next session the obnoxious bill was repealed, and a *per diem* allowance of eight dollars substituted in place of the salary.

During the course of the ensuing session, a subject came before the House which excited the enthusiasm of many of the members, and of none so much as that of Clay. It was in regard to South America, in her struggles for independence. We can not be expected to understand the feelings inspired at the time, by the events to which we refer. We have seen how "lame and impotent" the "conclusion" of that, which promised so fairly. We have been led to regard, with something of pity and contempt, the republics which have been formed from the fragments of the dismembered colonies of Spain. We have seen them ever in a ferment; never enjoying "the bliss of calm;" never reaching the true end of Government. We have seen their beautiful theory of liberty give way in practice, sometimes to anarchy, and sometimes to military despotism. We have seen them set forth in the career of self-government, with sounding manifestoes and every semblance of energy, only to relapse into hopeless supineness, and to become mere ciphers in the political interests of the world.

But when they began their struggles, only the brilliance of what they attempted was seen; the inauspicious ending was hidden in the future. The ardent and impulsive saw, in their declaration and struggle for liberty, a case parallel to our own. For a time it was fondly believed that the whole western hemisphere would become the home of liberty.

The temperament and feelings of Clay were of just the nature to be fired by such a spectacle. The theme was admirably adapted to his style of eloquence. Of Liberty in its largest and broadest sense, he was a devout worshiper; upon it, he might expend any measure of enthusiasm; without restriction, he might indulge in his loftiest declamation. He was untiring in his efforts to secure, from our Government, a recognition of South American independence. His speeches were translated into Spanish, and read at the head of the republican armies. He was regarded by the struggling colonies, as their champion in the American Congress. They voted him thanks, and corresponded with him through their generals. Yet the object at which he aimed was not immediately attained. Two or three years still elapsed, before the independence of the South American republics was recognized by our Government.

CHAPTER VI.

Mr. CLAY is offered the post of Minister to Russia—Also, a place in the Cabinet—Advocates internal improvements—Mr. CLAY the father of a policy and a party—The character and services of the Whig party—Seminole war—The conduct of Jackson.

MR. MADISON acknowledged the merit and abilities of Mr. CLAY, by offering him, upon his return from Europe, after the treaty of peace, the situation of Minister to Russia, and again, upon the occurrence of a vacancy in his Cabinet, the Secretaryship of War. Thus honors poured in upon the rising statesman, from every quarter. Success had smiled upon him from the first. By none of the artifices of the demagogue; by no special solicitation of any kind, he had risen to such estimation, that honors, instead of being sought by him, might almost be said to have come to him soliciting acceptance.

He declined the flattering offers of Mr. Madison, believing that he could serve his country best in her halls of legislation. He had occasion soon to advocate, what was ever with him, a favorite measure. It had been proposed to expend the *bonus* of the United States Bank, upon Internal Improvements. A bill to that effect was passed by Congress, but to the surprise of Mr. CLAY, was vetoed by President Madison.

This was upon the third of March, 1817. Upon the next day James Monroe was inaugurated President. But he, it was understood, would follow, in respect to this matter, in the footsteps of his predecessors. A resolution was, notwithstanding, offered in the House of Representatives, to the effect that Congress possessed the constitutional power to construct military roads, post roads and canals.

THE LIFE OF HENRY CLAY. 55

Upon this resolution CLAY, March thirteenth, made one of his most powerful and effective speeches. Political sentiment, from the day on which the Constitution was adopted until the present hour, has been divided as to the right which that instrument confers, to carry on systems of improvement within the different States, at the expense, and under the direction of the Federal Government.

The prosecution of such improvements, the advocates of State Rights have regarded an unwarrantable assumption of power, and an interference with the domestic polity of the different sovereignties which constitute the Republic. To yield the point, they have felt would be to advance far toward that consolidation of power, which they have ever earnestly deprecated.

Mr. CLAY expended the principal force of his argument against that class of objectors. He undertook to show that, if the power to carry on internal improvements was not expressly conferred by the Constitution, it was most unquestionably implied. The power to *establish* post roads, which was granted by the Constitution, was, he contended, the power to *construct* them.

The Government, he also argued, since it had the power to make war, had also, by implication, the power "to employ the whole physical means of the nation to render the war, whatever may be its character, successful and glorious." There was, therefore, "a direct and intimate relation between the power to make war and military roads and canals."

Some of his opponents might, perhaps, in view of his ingenuity, quote against him the story which, in earlier days, he brought forward against those who sought a warrant in the Constitution for a national bank. They might remind him of the Virginia justice, who represented "to the man, whose turkey had been stolen, that his books of precedents furnished no form for his case, but then he would grant him a precept to search for a cow, and, when looking for that, he might possibly find his turkey." They might charge him with being recreant to his early principles and possessed of an unequaled facility, both in changing his opinions, and confuting his own arguments.

It doubtless must be admitted, that Mr. Clay's views of the Constitution, during a course of years, underwent a change. He was less a States' Rights man than at first. By his political sagacity, he saw how much for the country a vigorous central power, well administered, might accomplish. He saw that to limit the Constitution, as some desired to limit it, would render that instrument a most effete and worthless thing. He saw that the tendency of the States' Rights doctrine was to rob us of our unity, in which resides our strength, and to substitute for it the weakness of jealous and conflicting sovereignties. He saw the great resources of our country, and he longed to develop them. Those resources, he felt, could not be made productive, unless Government reached out to them its arm of strength. A little more of federalism he, therefore, ingrafted upon his early democracy; but it was because the good and glory of his country pointed him to such a course. He was such a leader as the times demanded,—one to inaugurate a more united and vigorous policy. The country was undergoing a salutary political change, and it was given him to be the master-spirit of that change. His measures constituted him the founder and leader of a new party. That party, bearing long the old and honored name of Whig, is now, in all that is distinctive, passing away; but it would be wrong, either to measure the extent of its influence, by the length of its years, or to believe that it has passed the autumn of its decline, without accomplishing the mission for which it was called into existence. Most of the measures, which constituted its favorite policy, have, indeed, been permitted quietly to pass from notice, but not before they subserved, some of them at least, the valuable temporary ends for which they were designed; and not before others exerted upon the legislation of the country a formative influence, which, if not so great as was aimed at, is yet too decided to be effaced. As each year makes more apparent the vigor and efficiency of our noble Government; as each year reveals new proofs of the wonderful resources of our country; as each year gladdens our land with prosperity, and pours into our coffers no stinted tide of wealth, let not the agency of the Whig party, in accomplishing the glad result, be forgotten, and let not fitting honors be refused to the memory of their gallant leader, "Harry Clay."

The views upon internal improvements, which Mr. Clay advocated, on the thirteenth of March, he had the satisfaction of seeing sustained by Congress. The resolution was adopted by a vote of ninety to seventy-five. His labors, at different periods, for kindred objects, rendered him, in many sections of the country, the most popular man of the nation. At a prominent point upon the Cumberland road, which was constructed mainly through his influence, a stone, inscribed with his name, was erected to commemorate the gratitude of the people.

In 1818, Mr. Clay came into conflict, for the first time, with his future adversary,—"the man of iron will." General Jackson had been sent with an army, to repress disturbances occasioned by the Seminole Indians. In the discharge of his duty, he paid but little regard to the usages of civilized warfare. The unfortunate savages received, at his hands, such treatment as might be given to pirates or wild beasts. Two traders, Arbuthnot and Ambrister, were hung in violation of the rules of war. Several Spanish fortresses, though we were at peace with Spain, were attacked and taken.

A resolution of censure was moved in the House of Representatives. It became the occasion of a most exciting and stormy debate. Jackson was at the summit of popularity, as the hero of New Orleans. Yet Clay did not hesitate to characterize his conduct, in the terms which it deserved.

"To you, Mr. Chairman," said he, in the conclusion of his speech, "belongs the high privilege of transmitting, unimpaired, to posterity the fair character and liberty of our country. Do you expect to execute this high trust, by trampling, or suffering to be trampled down, law, justice, the Constitution, and the rights of the people?—by exhibiting examples of inhumanity, and cruelty, and ambition? When the minions of despotism heard, in Europe, of the seizure of Pensacola, how did they chuckle, and chide the admirers of our institutions, tauntingly pointing to the demonstration of a spirit of injustice and aggrandizement, made by our country in the midst of an amicable negotiation. Behold, said they, the conduct of those who are constantly reproaching kings. You saw how those admirers were astounded and hung their heads. You saw, too, when that illustrious man, who presides over us, adopted his pacific, moderate, and just course, how they once more lifted up their heads, with exultation and delight beaming on their countenances. And you saw how those minions, themselves, were finally compelled to unite in the general praises bestowed upon our government. Beware how you forfeit this exalted character. Beware how you give a fatal sanction, in this infant period of our Republic, scarcely yet two score years old, to military insubordination. Remember that Greece had her Alexander, Rome her Cæsar, England her Cromwell, France her Bonaparte, and that if we would escape the rock on which they split, we must avoid their errors.

"How different has been the treatment of General Jackson, and that modest but heroic young man, a native of one of the smallest States in the Union, who achieved for his country, on Lake Erie, one of the most glorious victories of the late war. In a moment of passion, he forgot himself and offered an act of violence, which was repented of as soon as perpetrated. He was tried, and suffered the judgment to be pronounced by his peers. Public justice was thought even then not to be satisfied. The press and Congress took up the subject. My honorable friend from Virginia (Mr. Johnson), the faithful and consistent sentinel of the law and of the Constitution, disapproved in that instance, as he does in this, and moved an inquiry. The public mind remained agitated and unappeased, until the recent atonement, so honorably made by the gallant Commodore. And is there to be a distinction between the officers of the two branches of the public service? Are former services, however eminent, to preclude even inquiry into recent misconduct? Is there to be no limit, no prudential bounds to the national gratitude? I am not disposed to censure the President for not ordering a court of inquiry, or a general court-martial. Perhaps impelled by a sense of gratitude, he determined, by anticipation, to extend to the General that pardon, which he had the undoubted right to grant after sentence. Let us not shrink from our duty. Let us assert our constitutional powers, and vindicate the instrument from military violation."

The popularity of Jackson, however, and the tacit influence of the Executive availed to prevent the passage of the resolution of censure.

CLAY, at the opening of his speech, had expressly disclaimed the influence of any personal prejudice.

"In rising to address you, Mr. Chairman," he had said, "on the very interesting subject which now engages the attention of Congress, I must be allowed to say, that all influences drawn from the course, which it will be my painful duty to take in this discussion, of unfriendliness, either to the chief magistrate of the country, or to the illustrious military chieftain, whose operations are under investigation, will be wholly unfounded. Toward that distinguished captain, who shed so much glory on our country,—whose renown constitutes so great a portion of its moral property,—I never had, I never can have any other feelings than those of the most profound respect and of the utmost kindness."

But this disavowal was not sufficient to avert the anger of the irascible General. He took deep offense at the course pursued by CLAY. Upon visiting Washington, which he did soon after, he refused to hold any communication with him. From this point, therefore, we date the beginning of the war between the political chieftains.

CHAPTER VII.

Mr. Clay as a "pacificator"—Missouri desires admission—Violent agitation of slavery—The Compromise—The efforts of Mr. Clay.

Mr. Clay's talents, during twenty years, had been displayed in various forms of legislation. One position remained to be tried before his character, as a statesman and patriot, might be pronounced complete. The opportunity soon presented itself. A struggle, not between this and other Governments, but the more fearful throes of civil dissension, occupied the public thought, and gave alarm to all the well-wishers of our institutions. Clay's services, for the first time, were demanded to pacify fraternal strife. He had earned laurels of which he might be proud in other and varied capacities, but so well did he acquit himself in this, so pre-eminently did he attract all eyes to himself, as to the only one who could accomplish what others despaired of; and so successfully, more than once afterward, did he perform the same benignant office, that no title seems so entirely to befit him as that by which he has sometimes been designated,—"The Great Pacificator."

The event which first revealed him to the country, in the capacity of which we speak, was what has been called the Missouri Question. As early as 1818, the Territory of Missouri intimated a desire to be admitted to the privileges of a State. The subject was taken up in Congress, in the session of 1818–19. The bill relating to the subject became the occasion of the most violent excitement, upon the vexed question of Slavery. The House of Representatives inserted in it the following resolutions, which were incorporated by a small majority:

"*Resolved*, That the further introduction of slavery, or involuntary servitude, be prohibited, except for the punishment of crimes, whereof the party shall have been fully convicted.

"And, that all children, born within the said State, after the admission thereof into the Union, shall be free at the age of twenty-five years."

The bill, as amended, was rejected by the Senate, and Missouri was condemned to wait. In the meantime popular feeling became greatly roused. In no amiable mood, at the next session of Congress, Missouri renewed her application. The subject was again taken up. Various resolutions were reported. It was moved, "that a committee be appointed to report a bill, prohibiting the further introduction of slaves, into the Territories of the United States, west of the Mississippi." This motion met with violent opposition. At last a compromise was agreed upon, in a conference of the two Houses of Congress. The terms of that compromise are conveyed in the following resolution:

"*Resolved*, That in all the Territory, ceded by France to the United States, under the name of Louisiana, which lies north of thirty-six degrees and thirty minutes, north latitude, not included within the limits contemplated by this act, slavery and involuntary servitude, otherwise than in the punishment of crimes, whereof the parties shall have been duly convicted, shall be, and is, hereby, forever prohibited: *Provided always*, That any person escaping into the same, from whom labor or service is lawfully claimed, in any State or Territory of the United States, such fugitive may be lawfully reclaimed, and conveyed to the person claiming his or her labor, or service, as aforesaid."

During the summer of 1820, the people of Missouri organized a State government, but, inflamed by the opposition which their application had met with, and the restrictions which it had been sought to impose upon them, inserted in their Constitution, a clause to the effect, that "it should be the duty of the General Assembly, as soon as possible, to pass such laws as might be necessary, to prevent free negroes and mulattoes from coming to, or settling in, the State, under any pretext whatever."

The committees, in both Houses of Congress, reported in

favor of sanctioning the Constitution, as it was. The Senate concurred, but the House was again distracted with intense excitement, and involved in a most stormy debate.

Nor was the excitement confined to Congress. It had become general throughout the country. The North was arrayed against the South, and the South against the North. Inflammatory meetings were held, and every newspaper teemed with new appeals to feelings already unduly exasperated.

The obnoxious clause was looked upon as inserted, in defiance of the North, and the restriction upon free negroes was held to conflict with the Constitution and the rights of citizenship. The true cause of excitement was, however, back of all this.

The public feeling, during the past few years, has been so often and so deeply agitated, in regard to the subject of slavery, that all other issues have become subordinate to it. It is the great social and political problem of our country. The Missouri question only furnished an occasion, for the outworking of a feeling, which is ever waiting to be roused. Upon one side of an invisible, but accurately defined line, stands an army of watchful opponents of slavery. Upon the other, the guardians of that institution, jealous of their privileges and ceaselessly on the alert against their invasion. Every thing, which promises the advance, most of all the predominance, of one of these lynx-eyed parties, brings against it, with angry menace, the other. The control of the legislation of the country, is the goal, toward which are bent the persistent efforts of both. The application for admission of every new State, therefore, which, by any possibility, whether of situation or of climate, can become an object of contention, develops their latent activities, and agitates with dangerous convulsions the country.

The application of Missouri occasioned so unusual an excitement, because its admission involved a test question, and would constitute a significant precedent. All of the territory of the Union, from which States previously had been formed, had had their domestic polity, so far as slavery was concerned, definitely settled by the action of the central Government. The ordinance of 1787 secured them to freedom.

But the case of Missouri was different. The new State was formed from a part of that territory which had been ceded, by France, to the United States. The destiny of that immense country became, therefore, an anxious problem. In respect to it there was no specific regulation of our Government. Was it, then, open to all the institutions of our country, not excepting the sectional one of the South; or, as the national domain, was it to be considered exclusively the property of freedom ? This was the exciting question, and, upon its solution, were involved immense results. If secured to the North alone, that section would receive thereby an inevitable predominance;—if open to both, the South might possibly maintain a political equality. The North argued, that it was contrary to the intentions of the founders of our Government; contrary to the genius of our institutions; and contrary to the rights of man, to extend slavery over a square foot of territory beyond its original limits. The South contended, that slavery already existed in the disputed territory; that it was an institution of the soil, by the previous legislation of another power; and that the slave States had equal right, with the non-slaveholding, to extend their institutions, and to enjoy their special privileges in any part of the national domain.

Mr. CLAY, during previous sessions, while the subject was before Congress, labored heroically to reconcile the painful differences. Private embarrassments compelled him, in 1820, to resign his office as Speaker, and to betake himself again to the practice of his profession. But the threatening attitude of affairs did not permit him to remain away long. Leaving behind the lesser concerns of private interest, he resumed his seat in Congress. This was in January, 1821.

His undoubted patriotism, his tried integrity, his unrivaled popularity, pointed him out as the arbiter of the strife. On the second of February, he procured the appointment of a committee of thirteen, of which he was Chairman. The committee reported the following resolution :

"*Resolved*, That the State of Missouri be admitted into the Union, on an equal footing with the original States, in all respects whatever, *upon the fundamental condition*, that the said State shall never pass any law, preventing any description of persons from coming to, and settling in, the said State, who now are, or may hereafter become, citizens of any of the States of this Union; and *provided also*, That the Legislature of the said State, by a solemn public act, shall declare the assent of the said State to the said fundamental condition, and shall transmit to the President of the United States, on or before the fourth Monday in November next, an authentic copy of the said act, upon the receipt whereof, the President, by proclamation, shall announce the fact; whereupon, and without any further proceeding on the part of Congress, the admission of said State into the Union shall be considered as complete; and *provided further*, That nothing herein contained, shall be construed to take from the State of Missouri, when admitted into the Union, the exercise of any right or power, which can now be constitutionally exercised, by any of the original States."

This resolution, however, notwithstanding the most eloquent and impassioned appeals of CLAY, was rejected in committee of the whole, and afterward in the House.

Soon after, the House was the scene of increased excitement. The occasion was the counting of the electoral votes for President. The interest turned upon the decision of the question, whether the votes from Missouri should be received. The Senate, which had assembled in joint-meeting with the House, withdrew. Great confusion and perplexity prevailed in consequence of an uncertainty, which Randolph had raised, as to the validity of the election, in the existing attitude of Missouri.

Difficulties seemed still, as far as ever from an amicable adjustment. Both parties were wearied with the conflict, and in despair as to its result.

Mr. CLAY made another effort. He offered to the House the following resolution:

"*Resolved*, That a committee be appointed, on the part of the House, jointly with such committee as may be appointed on the part of the Senate, to consider and report to the Senate, and to the House, respectively, whether it be expedient, or not, to make provision for the admission of Missouri into the Union, on the same footing as the original States; and for the due execution of the laws, within Missouri; and, if not, whether any other, and what provision, adapted to her actual condition, ought to be made by law."

The House adopted the resolution. The committee consisted of twenty-three members. Mr. CLAY exerted himself to have those appointed, whom he knew to be willing to compromise the difficulty, and give peace to the country. He himself was at the head of the number. The Senate appointed a committee to confer with that of the House. They met in joint-conference, and adopted a report not greatly varying from that which had been previously presented by the committee of thirteen.

But the country, wearied by the long agitation, was heartily desirous of peace. The report, when laid before the House, was adopted by a vote of eighty-seven to eighty-one. Missouri acquiesced in it, and thus, at last, was settled the question, which threatened, at one time, to rend asunder the Union, and kindle the flames of civil war.

The nation has always accorded to Mr. CLAY its gratitude, for bringing about this happy result; but how deeply we are in his debt, those only can know who witnessed his persevering labors; who were aware of his sleepless and incessant anxiety; and who listened to the impassioned, and often pathetic tones of his eloquence.

CHAPTER VIII.

Candidates for the Presidency in 1824—No election by the people—Mr. CLAY's influence given to Mr. Adams—Charge of corruption—Mr. Kremer of Pennsylvania—Revival of the charge by Jackson—More trouble—A duel with Randolph.

NOTHING unusual, either in his personal history, or in the interests of his country, interrupted, for the two or three years subsequent to the events which we have described, the even tenor of Mr. CLAY's life. Between his professional employment, domestic ease, and the toils of legislation, he passed his time until the Presidential canvass of 1824. His abilities and popularity had long pointed significantly toward the Presidency. His admirers waited only for him to attain the proper age and experience, to bring forward his claims.

Jackson, Crawford and John Quincy Adams were before the people for their votes. The friends of CLAY believed that his time, too, had fully come. Several State Legislatures had expressed their preference for him. Kentucky, two years in advance, had promised to stand by him.

The canvass went duly on, but resulted in the election of no one of the four candidates. Jackson stood highest on the list, Adams next, and CLAY the last. The three highest only could be presented to the House for their choice. It devolved, therefore, upon CLAY to decide upon which he would bestow his vote and influence. Meanwhile, he was the object of marked attention from the adherents of the several opposing aspirants for honor. His own personal preferences were for Mr. Crawford, but such was the state of Crawford's health, that he believed him unfitted for the duties of the Presidency. Jackson and Adams he believed to be, practically, the only candidates, between whom he was called to choose. He gave the preference to Mr. Adams, and thus secured his election. Upon assuming the Presidential chair, Mr. Adams offered to Mr. Clay a seat in his Cabinet as Secretary of State. This office Mr. Clay accepted.

Such is the brief history of an occurrence, which party malignity afterward converted into an instrument, which, when he was at the full tide of his popularity, well-nigh proved fatal to the reputation of Clay. Never before had he felt the blasting breath of calumny, nor taken any abiding lessons in the school of adversity. Confident in the integrity of his own character, trusting to the firmness of an established reputation, he committed what he afterward acknowledged to be the blunder of his life. The finger of suspicion was pointed at him, and through many a long year, his fortunes underwent a disastrous eclipse.

Time has done for him what his own assertions could not do. His character is thoroughly vindicated. It is doubtful, whether the bitterest enemy he ever had, while living, now believes him guilty of corruption in the transaction for which he was reproached. It will not, therefore, be necessary to undertake a formal vindication of his character, but only to give a short and simple history of those proceedings which proposed, as their end, to blacken it.

We have said that, previous to the election in the House, Mr. Clay was made the subject of marked attentions, by the friends of the opposing candidates. "Every body," as he said, in an address to his constituents, "professed to regret, after I was excluded from the House, that I had not been returned to it. I seemed to be the favorite of every body. Describing my situation to a distant friend, I said to him, 'I am enjoying, while alive, the posthumous honors which are usually awarded to the venerated dead.' A person not acquainted with human nature, would have been surprised, in listening to these praises, that the object of them had not been elected by general acclamation. None made more or warmer manifestations of these sentiments of esteem and admiration, than some of the friends of General

Jackson. None were so reserved as those of Mr. Adams, under an opinion (as I have learned since the election), which they early imbibed, that the western vote would be influenced only by its own sense of public duty; and that, if its judgment pointed to any other than Mr. Adams, nothing which they could do would secure it to him. These professions and manifestations were taken by me, for what they were worth.

"I knew that the sunbeams would quickly disappear, after my opinion should be ascertained, and that they would be succeeded by a storm; although I did not foresee exactly how it would burst upon my poor head. I found myself transformed, from a candidate before the people, into an elector for the people. I deliberately examined the duties incident to this new attitude, and weighed all the facts before me, upon which my judgment was to be formed or reviewed. If the eagerness of any of the heated partisans of the respective candidates, suggested a tardiness in the declaration of my intention, I believed that the new relation, in which I was placed to the subject, imposed on me an obligation to pay some respect to delicacy and decorum.

"Meanwhile, that very reserve supplied aliment to newspaper criticism. The critics could not comprehend how a man standing as I had stood, toward the other gentlemen, should be restrained, by a sense of propriety, from instantly fighting under the banners of one of them, against the others. Letters were issued from the manufactory at Washington, to come back, after performing long journeys, for Washington consumption. These letters imputed to 'Mr. CLAY and his friends a mysterious air,—a portentous silence,' etc. From dark and distant hints, the progress was easy to open and bitter denunciation. Anonymous letters, full of menace and abuse, were almost daily poured in on me. Personal threats were communicated to me through friendly organs, and I was kindly apprized of all the glories of village effigies, which awaited me. A systematic attack was simultaneously commenced upon me, from Boston to Charleston, with an object, present and future, which it was impossible to mistake. No man but myself, could know the nature, extent, and variety of means which were employed to awe and influence me. I bore them, I trust, as *your* representative ought to have borne them, and as became me."

The friends of Jackson, at last, as it would seem, became convinced that, unless desperate measures were resorted to, Mr. Clay's vote and influence would be given to Mr. Adams. A new mode of intimidation was therefore adopted. A letter appeared in the Columbian Observer, published at Philadelphia, charging definitely upon Mr. Clay the terms of a bargain between himself and Mr. Adams, in accordance with which he was to support the latter, and receive, as his reward, the first seat in the Cabinet. The letter professed to be written by a member of Congress, acquainted with the facts which he affirmed.

Mr. Clay felt himself called upon to publish an indignant denial, and to brand the author of the letter, "as a base and infamous calumniator." The publication of this card, by Mr. Clay, called out one from Mr. Kremer of Pennsylvania. In it he avowed, "though somewhat equivocally, that he was the author of the letter to the Columbian Observer." "To Mr. Crowninshield, a member from Massachusetts, formerly Secretary of the Navy," continues Mr. Clay, in the address from which we have quoted, "he declared, that he was not the author of that letter. In his card he draws a clear line of separation, between my friends and me, acquitting them and undertaking to make good his charges in that letter, only so far as I was concerned. The purpose of this discrimination is obvious. At that time the election was undecided, and it was, therefore, as important to abstain from imputations against my friends, as it was politic to fix them upon me. If they could be made to believe that I had been perfidious, in the transport of their indignation, they might have been carried to the support of General Jackson.

"I received the National Intelligencer, containing Mr. Kremer's card, at breakfast, on the morning of its publication. As soon as I read the card, I took my resolution. The terms of it clearly implied, that it had not entered into his conception to have a personal affair with me, and I should justly have exposed myself to universal ridicule, if I had sought one with him. I determined to lay the matter before the House, and respectfully to invite an investigation of my conduct. I accordingly made a communication to the House, on the same day, the motives for which I assigned. Mr. Kremer was in his place, and, when I sat down, rose and stated, that he was ready and willing to substantiate his charges against me. This was his voluntary declaration, unprompted by his aiders and abettors, who had no opportunity of previous consultation with him, on that point. Here was an issue, publicly and solemnly joined, in which the accused invoked an inquiry into serious charges against him, and the accuser professed an ability and a willingness to establish them.

"A debate ensued, on the next day, which occupied the greater part of it, during which Mr. Kremer declared to Mr. Brent of Louisiana, a friend of mine, and to Mr. Little of Maryland, a friend of General Jackson, as they have certified, 'that he never intended to charge Mr. CLAY with corruption or dishonor, in his intended vote for Mr. Adams as President, or that he had transferred, or could transfer, the votes or interests of his friends; that he (Mr. Kremer) was among the last men in the nation to make such a charge against Mr. CLAY; and that his letter was never intended to convey the idea given to it.'"

A committee was appointed by the House, agreeably to the request of Mr. CLAY. It consisted of seven members, not one of whom was his political friend.

The committee "called upon Mr. Kremer to execute his pledge, publicly given, in his proper place, and also previously given in the public prints." "Mr. Kremer was stimulated by every motive which could impel to action; by his consistency of character; by duty to his constituents, to his country; by that of redeeming his solemn pledge; by his anxious wish for the success of his favorite, whose interests could not fail to be advanced by supporting his atrocious charges.

"But Mr. Kremer had now the benefit of the advice of his friends. He had no proofs, for the plainest of all reasons, because there was no truth in his charges. They saw that to attempt to establish them, and to fail, as he must fail in the attempt, might lead to an exposure of the conspiracy, of which he was the organ.

"They advised, therefore, that he should make a retreat, and their adroitness suggested, that, in an objection, to that jurisdiction of the House which had been admitted; and in the popular topics of the freedom of the press; *his* duty to his constituents; and the inequality in the condition of the Speaker of the House and a member on the floor, plausible means might be found to deceive the ignorant and conceal his disgrace.

"A labored communication was accordingly prepared by them, in Mr. Kremer's name, and transmitted to the committee, founded upon these suggestions. Thus the valiant champion who had boldly stepped forward and promised, as a representative of the people, to 'cry aloud and spare not,' forgot all his gratuitous gallantry and boasted patriotism, and sank, at once, into profound silence."

Shortly afterward, Mr. Adams was inducted into office, and appointed Mr. CLAY to the Department of State. The acceptance of office under the new administration gave substance, in the eyes of many, to the vague insinuations and charges, which, otherwise, would have passed away with the excitement of the political canvass. Mr. CLAY felt, afterward, that in that instance, he committed a mistake.

"I will take this occasion," said he in his speech, upon his retirement to private life, "to say, that I am, and have been long satisfied, that it would have been wiser and more politic in me, to have declined accepting the office of Secretary of State, in 1825. Not that my motives were not as pure and patriotic, as ever carried any man into public office. Not that the calumny, which was applied to the fact, was not as gross and unfounded as any that was ever propagated. Not that valued friends and highly esteemed opponents did not unite, in urging my acceptance of the office. Not that the administration of Mr. Adams will not, I sincerely believe, advantageously compare with that of any of his predecessors, in economy, purity, prudence and wisdom. Not that Mr. Adams was himself wanting, in any of those high qualifications, and upright and patriotic intentions, which were suited to the office. But my error, in accepting the office, arose out of my underrating the power of detraction and the force of ignorance, and abiding, with too sure a confidence, in the conscious integrity and uprightness of my own motives."

Well might he regret it, for, like an unquiet spirit, for years the charge of corruption was not permitted to rest. It was ever starting up to oppose his progress and to interrupt his peace of mind. When the public had almost ceased to speak of it, the hateful calumny was revived by an enemy who never faltered in the execution of any purpose, because of unnecessary scruples of conscience, and who, through his immense popularity could give to any "airy nothing, a local habitation and a name." General Jackson took up the slander. He perhaps believed it, for it is easy to believe what we wish to be true. The office out of which he had been disappointed, he determined yet to secure. But there were formidable competitors in his way. Those competitors must be removed. To accomplish that, no way was so effective as to blacken their characters. Report accused the Executive and the principal Secretary of corruption. There was, therefore, thus much ground to begin upon. An overture was conveyed to Jackson,—so he affirmed,—to make a bargain with Mr. CLAY before Mr. Adams should make it. The bearer * of the overture intimated that the latter intention was entertained, by the friends of the respective parties. The General,—as he himself asserts,—turned away in disdain from such a dishonorable proposal. "Before he would reach the Presi-

---

* In the following extract from a letter (dated Washington, August 14, 1827), to Francis Brooke, by Mr. CLAY, it may be seen who was the bearer of the overture, and what his relation to the matter:

"I hope you are not mistaken in the good effect of my Lexington speech. Mr. Buchanan has presented his communication to the public; and although he evidently labors throughout the whole of it to spare and cover General Jackson, he fails in every essential particular to sustain the General. Indeed, I could not desire a stronger statement from Mr. Buchanan. The tables are completely turned upon the General. Instead of any intrigues on my part and that of my friends, they were altogether on the side of General Jackson and his friends. But I will leave the

dential Chair, by such means of bargain and corruption, he would see the earth open, and swallow both Mr. Clay, and his friends, and himself with them."

"During the dispensation of the hospitalities of the Hermitage, in the midst of a mixed company of individuals, from various States, he permits himself," says Mr. Clay, "to make certain statements, respecting my friends and me, which, if true, would forever dishonor and degrade us. The words are hardly passed from his mouth, before they are committed to paper, by one of his guests, and transmitted, in the form of a letter, to another State, when they are published in a newspaper, and thence circulated throughout the Union. And now he pretends that these statements were made 'without any calculation that they were to be thrown into the public journals.' Does he reprove the indiscretion of this guest, who had violated the sanctity of a conversation at the hospitable board? Far from it. The public is incredulous. It can not be, General Jackson would be so

---

statement to your own reflections. I directed a copy to be inclosed yesterday to Mr. Southard. It must confirm any good impression produced by my speech."

The impression made by Mr. Buchanan's letter is still more apparent in the following communication of R. P. Letcher to Mr. Clay:

"Lancaster, August 27, 1827.

"My Dear Sir—Yours of the ninth instant came to hand last night. The one by Mr. A., I received a few days since by private hand, from the county of Harlan. With your letter of the ninth, Mr. Buchanan's response to the hero was received. This answer is well put together. As they say, in Connecticut, "there is a great deal of good reading" in Buck's reply. It is modest and genteel, yet strong and conclusive. I am truly delighted with the manner in which B. has acquitted himself. I really feared and believed he was placed in such a dilemma, by the General, that he could not extricate himself with any sort of credit. But he has come forth victoriously. I am greatly gratified with the result, and must believe it will have a happy effect upon the Presidential election. It is impossible it should turn out otherwise. Virginia, after this, will not— can not support the General. I never had the least hope of Virginia until now.

"I presume Buck's reply supersedes the necessity of any reference to the conversation in my room. I am glad of it."

wanting in delicacy and decorum. The guest appeals to him for the confirmation of the published statements, and the General promptly addresses him a letter, 'in which he unequivocally confirms' (says Mr. Carter Beverly *), 'all I have said, regarding the overture made to him, pending the last Presidential election before Congress; and he *asserts a great deal more than he ever told me.*'"

But other troubles grew out of the annoying slander. It was a favorite dream with CLAY, to establish, with the new South American republics, a great American alliance. Those republics had appointed a Congress, at Panama, to consult upon their mutual interests, in opposition to Spain. Mr. CLAY, who was now Secretary of State, desired that the United States should co-operate with them through a special representative. The

---

* In 1842, Carter Beverly did the following act of tardy justice to the reputation of Mr. CLAY:

"FREDERICKSBURG, VA., April 2, 1842.

"DEAR SIR—On my arrival here yesterday I received your reply to my letter of February last, from Middlesex, and feel glad to find that the communication I then made to you was well received, and kindly acknowledged.

"It is assuredly a matter of high satisfaction to me to believe, that I discharged the obligation which feeling and duty dictated, in doing the justice I designed, of effacing the indignity cast upon you by the unfortunate, and to me unhappy Fayetteville letter that was, and has been so much the subject of injury to you in the public mind. It is now, I trust, put entirely to rest in the minds of all honorable and candid men, of whatever political persuasion; for surely none can, or will henceforward presume to countenance the miserable slander that went forth in that communication to the public against you. The entire revocation of it given by me ought to overwhelm the author of it with utter shame and mortification; and if I had any right to say, were I in his situation, it would be my province, as it should be an incumbent duty on me, to make every atonement possible for such an unfounded, unprovoked attack upon your integrity and public fame.

"Believing that your letter to me, and this my reply, are calculated to benefit you in the public mind, I have sent both to 'The Richmond Whig' and 'Independent' for publication.

"I reiterate expressions of health and happiness to you, and remain yours, etc."

time seemed to him to have come for accomplishing his brilliant design. The President entered with enthusiasm into the project. Randolph, as usual, was found in the opposition. At the close of a characteristic speech, he denounced the concurrence of the President and Secretary, as "the coalition of Blifil and Black George,—of the puritan and blackleg."

Conflicts had not been unfrequent between Clay and Randolph. The latter, early in Clay's Congressional career, had taken exceptions to his rulings, as Speaker, and had published a card, which elicited from Mr. Clay a reply. More than once they had seemed upon the point of open rupture.

Perhaps, under ordinary circumstances, the insinuation of Randolph would have passed unnoticed, as one of that strange man's eccentricities of speech. But Clay felt that, now, he was not himself rich enough in reputation to be generous. His feelings, lacerated by the thousand stabs of calumny, writhed under the last infliction. He had borne heroically open detraction,— this covert sneer stung to the quick his proud and sensitive soul. He yielded to his angry impulse, and sent to Randolph a challenge.

Randolph accepted it. "I have no explanations to give," he exclaimed. "I will not give any. I am called to the field. I have agreed to go, and am ready to go." His unconciliatory disposition seemed like blood-thirstiness, but it is only justice to him to explain that it was not so.

"The night before the duel," says General James Hamilton of South Carolina, "Mr. Randolph sent for me. I found him calm, but in a singularly kind and confiding mood. He told me that he had something on his mind to tell me. He then remarked, 'Hamilton, I have determined to receive, without returning, Clay's fire; nothing shall induce me to harm a hair of his head; I will not make his wife a widow, or his children orphans. Their tears would be shed over his grave; but when the sod of Virginia rests on my bosom, there is not, in this wide world, one individual to pay this tribute upon mine."

When the parties, the next day, had taken their positions, Randolph's pistol was accidentally discharged before the word was given. "The moment this event took place, General Jesup, Mr. Clay's friend, called out that he would instantly leave the ground with his friend, if that occurred again. Mr. Clay, at once exclaimed, it was entirely an accident, and begged that the gentleman might be allowed to go on. On the word being given, Mr. Clay fired without effect, Mr. Randolph discharging his pistol in the air. The moment Mr. Clay saw that Mr. Randolph had thrown away his fire, with a gush of sensibility, he instantly approached Randolph and said, with an emotion which" (adds General Hamilton), "I can never forget, 'I trust in God, my dear sir, you are untouched; after what has occurred, I would not have harmed you for a thousand worlds.'"

Of dueling, Mr. Clay had, previously to this, spoken in the following terms: "I owe it to the community to say, that, whatever heretofore I may have done, or by inevitable circumstances might be forced to do, no man holds in deeper abhorrence, than I do, that pernicious practice. Condemned, as it must be, by the judgment and philosophy, to say nothing of the religion of every thinking man, it is an affair of feeling, about which we can not, although we should, reason. Its true corrective will be found, when all shall unite, as all ought to unite, in its unqualified proscription."

CHAPTER IX.

The Tariff of 1824—Question as to the expediency of a protective tariff—Difference between theory and practice—Unpopularity of the protective system at the South—Nullification—Mr. CLAY introduces his compromise tariff, and harmony is restored.

A BILL to protect American Industry was adopted by the House of Representatives, in 1820, but was lost in the Senate by a vote of twenty-two to twenty-one. In 1824, the committee on manufactures reported another bill, recommending a high protective tariff. Mr. CLAY had labored assiduously from the first to procure the adoption of such a measure. The reader will remember that his earlier Senatorial efforts were directed to that end. He made a forcible speech upon the subject, in 1820; but it was in 1824, that he laid out all his strength. His argument was extended and elaborate. He brought to the subject much and varied investigation. He equipped himself for an arduous parliamentary conflict, for, among his opponents, *primus inter pares*, stood Mr. Webster. The bill was successful. It passed both Houses of Congress, received the signature of the President and became a law.

While with one class in the community, the claims of Mr. CLAY, to be considered a patriot, have been based upon the advocacy of no measure, so much as upon that of the protective system, with another, his partiality for that very policy has been the occasion for calling in question his political sagacity and the soundness of his statesmanship. It has been justly said, that no system of doctrines can obtain extensive belief, without containing some element of truth. The converse is, perhaps, likewise true. No system prevails among fallible men, which does not contain some admixture of error. We may apply the axiom. A protective tariff is not the sublimation of wisdom, which some have regarded it; neither is it that offspring of delusion and folly, which it has seemed in the eyes of others. In theory, we are obliged to confess that such a tariff appears radically unsound. In practice, it assumes altogether another appearance. Such an assertion might seem strange, had it not been seen long ago, and in multiplied instances, that theory and practice do not necessarily nor always coincide.

Theories too often presuppose a state of things which does not exist. A thousand circumstances, prone to be disregarded because of their seeming insignificance, often demand, in practice, from their combined influence, unexpected modifications. The force of many influences, also, can not be calculated, until the experiment has been tried. A theory of political economy, moreover, which may suit one nation, or be fitting at a particular time, will not infallibly suit every other nation and be adapted to all times alike.

Because a protective tariff is not needed now, it is becoming common to suppose that it was always a useless and an absurd institution. Because the theory of protection is liable to serious objections, it is argued that, under all circumstances, it must be unphilosophical and impolitic.

But we say to the objector, that he proceeds too fast. His arguments are truly plausible, but they presuppose a state of things which does not exist,—which never has existed. They proceed too much upon the fallacious ground, that this is a perfect world, and that the nations of it bear toward each other the relation of a united, confiding, unselfish brotherhood. If this supposition were true, then a protective tariff would be to the last degree absurd and mischievous. But unfortunately it is the furthest possible from being true.

Upon the supposition of the theorizer, the argument which is regarded the strongest against protection would be absolutely unanswerable. This argument is, that each nation should devote itself to that branch of industry, in which it can engage with the most facility, and to which its natural advantages most clearly point. If that be agriculture, then let agriculture flourish; if it be commerce, then let commerce reign; if manufactures, then let workshops abound; but let nothing be forced into a premature existence, for thereby risk will be incurred,—danger of continual frost to the hot-house plants which you have reared; or else at special expense they must be shielded,—expense bringing no return, but ending in inevitable loss.

This reasoning would do if all governments were Utopias;—if the rule, to love our neighbor as ourselves, was recognized and obeyed in the intercourse of nations; but who does not know, that a thousand of the expenses of government arise from the fact that the opposite of all this is true? Who does not know that it would, according to theory, be infinitely better for a nation's wealth and prosperity, to disband its armies, to dismantle its forts, to convert into trading vessels its ships of war? But who would advise the experiment? Who does not see that certain tendencies belonging to depraved humanity, brand it as impracticable?

Each nation, in this selfish world, must stand upon the defensive; each must in a measure contain within itself all needed resources; each must be capable, when occasion, which is not unfrequent, requires to occupy an attitude of self-dependence; each nation must, in short, be a microcosm, where all the pursuits of men, to a greater or less extent, shall be followed, and where, for all their absolute wants, there shall be suitable provision.

A country may, from circumstances of climate and soil, be plainly pointed to agriculture, as the surest source of its wealth; but a country exclusively agricultural is plunged into the deepest embarrassment and distress, when war intercepts the supplies of commerce, and withholds the products of the workshop. Another country, finding but a scanty subsistence from its barren hillsides, may see the finger of Providence pointing to running streams and commodious harbors, as adapted to do that for its prosperity, which an unkindly soil refuses to do; but the instinct of self-defense forbids an exclusive attention to manufactures and trade, lest sudden hostilities should confront the people with starvation.

Thus the theory of legislation is modified by unavoidable and dangerous contingencies. A system of safeguards and checks upon dishonesty, often complicated and perplexing, but confessedly necessary, governs the daily business dealings of men. Nations are but collections of men of like passions, and for their mutual security must, therefore, submit to a similar control.

But in some instances, and the earlier condition of our country constituted one of such, other arguments plead for a protective system with special power. War produces for an agricultural people the results that we have indicated. The foreign supply is cut off. The demand is, however, imperative, and domestic labor is called upon to supply the deficiency. Manufactories, therefore, spring up upon every hand, and, if hostilities are long continued, draw to themselves a large amount of the labor and capital of the country. No part of the country, as it often happens, is more benefited by this direction of industry, or more imperatively demands it, than the agricultural.

But peace returns and brings back the abundant products of the foreign loom and anvil. Domestic fabrics are driven from the market by perhaps a better article, furnished at a cheaper price. Hence, an interesting question rises at once for solution: Shall the immense capital embarked in manufactures be exposed to inevitable shipwreck, or shall Government extend to it a while the protection which peace has suddenly withdrawn?

Meanwhile, those who had been benefited begin to complain. It is hard, they say, that we, who have nothing whatever to do with the workshop, should be compelled to bear the burden of its support, and be forced to take an inferior article at an exorbitant price. But the complaint, though plausible, is founded upon a forgetfulness of benefits absolutely essential, already received, and upon a forgetfulness that obligations are mutual;— that it would be wrong to devote to destruction, at the moment they cease to receive benefit from it, that capital which, by their own wants and importunity, was directed into its existing channels. The argument is supported, also, by the consideration, that the demanded protection is only a temporary expedient; that it is not absolute and indefinite support which is asked for, but, just for the present, a little "material aid."

The problem of a protective policy, therefore, it will be seen, resolves itself into a very different question from this: Shall a country, prematurely and without occasion, quicken into life manufactures by a protective tariff? The true question is more generally a double one, namely: First, shall a country, by its variety of interests, be ready for a healthful self-dependence? Secondly, when by unavoidable contingencies a new and important interest is created, shall it be crushed out of existence the moment that it ceases to be profitable, when by a little encouragement, it might, at no remote period, instead of needing assistance, become a right arm of strength?

In our own country, the manufacturing interest received a powerful impulse by the war of 1812. Shortly after the close of hostilities, John C. Calhoun advocated a tariff designed to confer protection upon it. We must consider it an act of liberal and enlightened statesmanship in him, for to his own state the benefit was not so much to accrue, as to a distant section, characterized by different institutions. The tariff law of 1816 extended encouragement to manufactures, without elevating them into a monopoly, or stimulating them unduly by excessive protection. The tariff of 1824 can not, we fear, plead entire innocence of such an imputation.

National pride is easily provoked to go too far. It was a fond ambition of Mr. CLAY to render his country independently great. Seeing the immense resources of every kind, of which it could boast, he believed that it might reach its full measure of prosperity by inward development. He, therefore, advocated a system of protection which should result in the exclusion of foreign competition. But this was to exalt the means above the end; it was to stimulate, which is injurious, rather than to protect; it was to push manufactures beyond their proper limits; to create a monopoly; to subordinate the interests of trade to the interests of the workshop; to aim, in a prejudicial way, at independence, which is unattainable, rather than at self-dependence, which is both attainable and desirable.

The consequence was, that while one section of the country and one powerful monied interest were loud in their praises of the protective system, and eager to retain it, another section and another interest murmured against it as unjust and oppressive, and threatened, unless it were repealed, to employ the most extreme measures of redress.

South-Carolina especially denounced the law as unconstitutional and odious; threatened to disregard it, and entered upon a course which bore the appearance of open rebellion.

General Jackson was at the head of Government. He detested the law almost as much as South-Carolina, but since it was a law, he determined that, at all hazards, it should be obeyed. Inflammatory meetings were held at Charleston. Open resistance to the officers of Government was recommended. Materials for war were collected. Meanwhile United States troops were sent to the disaffected State. Jackson, it was believed, would bombard, at the least provocation, the city of Charleston, and hang as traitors Hayne, Calhoun, and others of the leaders. Intense excitement pervaded the country.

Randolph, broken down with age and yet more by disease, was roused by the sounds of coming strife. "Lifted into his carriage like an infant," says his biographer, "he went from county to county, and spoke with a power that effectually aroused the slumbering multitudes." "In the course of his speech at Buckingham, he is reported to have said, 'Gentlemen, I am filled with the most gloomy apprehensions for the fate of the Union. I can not express to you how deeply I am penetrated with a sense of the danger, which, at this moment, threatens its existence. If Madison filled the Executive chair, he might be bullied into some compromise. If Monroe was in power, he might be coaxed into some adjustment of this difficulty. But Jackson is obstinate, headstrong, and fond of fight. I fear matters must come to an open rupture. If so, this Union is gone!' Then pausing for near a minute, raising his finger in that emphatic manner, so peculiar to his action as a speaker, and seeming, as it were, to breathe more freely, he continued,—'There is one man, and one man only, who can save this Union,—that man is HENRY CLAY. I know he has the power. I believe he will be found to have the patriotism and firmness equal to the occasion.'"

Mr. Randolph was not mistaken. Mr. Clay proved himself to have alike "the power," "the patriotism," and the "firmness." Several years had elapsed between the passage of the tariff bill of 1824, and the events which we are describing. Various modifications had been introduced. Meanwhile Mr. Clay had retired from his seat in the cabinet, had returned to his home, and by his grateful State had been again sent to the national councils. He was now in the Senate. Advocating still his favorite policy, he came forward in January, 1832, with the following resolution:

"*Resolved*, That the existing duties upon articles imported from foreign countries, and not coming into competition with similar articles made or produced within the United States, ought to be forthwith abolished, except the duties upon wines and silks, and that those ought to be reduced; and that the committee on finance be instructed to report a bill accordingly."

A bill, framed according to this resolution, was adopted in July, 1832. But every measure which avowed protection as its object, was regarded by the opponents of the system unconstitutional. The opposition increased, especially throughout the Southern States. At least South-Carolina assumed the attitude which we have described.

At this juncture, Mr. Clay evinced how great and unselfish was his patriotism. In the language of one, who was not a political friend, " with parental fondness, he cherished his American System,—with unyielding pertinacity, contended for it to the last extremity;—but, when it became a question between that and the integrity of the Union, he did not hesitate; like Abraham, he was ready to sacrifice his own offspring on the altar of his country, and to see the fond idols he had cherished perish one by one before his lingering eyes."

He introduced a bill which received the name of the Compromise Tariff Bill. From it, for the sake of his country's peace, he excluded most of those features which were odious to the South, however fondly they had been cherished by himself. Yet it was truly a compromise, for the enemies of his system had also introduced a bill designed to be destructive of protection. The new tariff bill of Mr. CLAY provided for a gradual reduction of duties, until 1842, at which time the rate was to continue at twenty per centum until further legislation. His sacrifice was not unavailing. The bill received the approval of both Houses of Congress, was signed by the President, and became a law, March, 1833.

Thus the country, which to all human appearances had been upon the verge of civil war, was again rescued from its danger by the firmness and the patriotism of HENRY CLAY.

CHAPTER X.

Mr. Clay is again defeated as a candidate for the Presidency—Clay and Jackson as rival leaders—Removal of the Deposits by the President—Mr. Clay's indignant opposition—Resolutions of censure—The Cherokees—Lavish expenditure—The expunging resolution—The sub-treasury bill—Dawning of better times.

In 1831, Mr. Clay was nominated by his friends for the Presidency, but slander had accomplished its intended work. Jackson, his opponent, was borne into office by an immense majority.

But this was not the whole of his defeat. It was the special labor of the Executive to undo all the long-cherished, long-struggled-for measures of Mr. Clay. The veto power was used with unprecedented frequency. First, a bill which had been passed to renew the Charter of the United States Bank, returned with the President's negative. This was followed by the rejection of a bill, adopted by large majorities, for the distribution of the Public Lands among the several States. The system, in short, which with infinite pains and with a lifetime of labor, Mr. Clay had succeeded in building up, he now saw remorselessly overthrown. His iron-willed opponent had seized him at an advantage, and seemed determined to make the most of his triumph. Mr. Clay ruled still with almost resistless sway in Congress, but what availed it, when, a short mile from the Capitol, sat one who, with a dash of his pen, could undo the result of weeks of legislation. Mr. Clay in the Senate murmured against the veto power, but the Constitution conferred it, and what could be done but to submit.

But not even here did the President stop. Not content with the unlimited use of constitutional privileges, he overstepped the prescribed bounds, and made use of what his most devoted admirers must acknowledge to be, at least, doubtful prerogatives.

Congress, in March, 1833, had declared by special resolution, that the Government Deposits, in the opinion of the House, might safely be continued in the Bank of the United States. But the President had determined that they should be removed, and when was he known to hesitate in the execution of any measure upon which he had decided? The Secretary of the Treasury was directed to remove them. In the face of the action of Congress and the express terms of the Constitution defining his duties, he would not obey. The President dismissed him from his cabinet and substituted in his place the Attorney General, Mr. Taney. The new Secretary was more compliant. He issued the necessary directions, and the Deposits were removed.

Congress was outraged. The action of the President met with a loud burst of indignation. The military despotism which Mr. Clay had deprecated, when he alluded to the course of Jackson in the Seminole war, seemed about to be established. Mr. Clay stood forth as the champion of the opposition. He introduced resolutions of censure, and supported them by a powerful speech. The war between the two most inflexible and popular men of the nation was fairly joined and at its hight. Clay gained, apparently, the victory. The resolutions of censure were adopted, but the victory was only in appearance. Little did Jackson regard resolutions of censure, when his mind was settled upon the propriety of any course. He was not to be crushed by words. He moved on, as though nothing had happened.

The violence done to the financial interests of the country occasioned deep embarrassments. Petitions poured in from every quarter. Mr. Clay again was in the van and the thickest of the fight. To the President of the Senate, Mr. Van Buren, he addressed himself in terms of eloquent entreaty and remonstrance. 'In twenty-four hours,' said he, 'the executive branch could adopt a measure which would afford an efficacious and substantial remedy, and re-establish confidence. And those who, in this chamber, support the administration, could not render a better service than to repair to the executive mansion, and, placing before the chief magistrate the naked and undisguised truth, prevail upon him to retrace his steps and abandon his fatal experiment. No one, sir, can perform that duty with more propriety than yourself. You can, if you will, induce him to change his course. To you, then, sir, in no unfriendly spirit, but with feelings softened and subdued by the deep distress which pervades every class of our countrymen, I make the appeal. By your official and personal relations with the President, you maintain with him an intercourse which I neither enjoy nor covet. Go to him and tell him, without exaggeration, but in the language of truth and sincerity, the actual condition of his bleeding country. Tell him it is nearly ruined and undone, by the measures which he has been induced to put in operation. Tell him that *his* experiment is operating on the nation like the philosopher's experiment upon a convulsed animal in an exhausted receiver, and that it must expire in agony, if he does not pause, give it free and sound circulation, and suffer the energies of the people to be revived and restored.

"Tell him that in a single city more than sixty bankruptcies, involving a loss of upward of fifteen millions of dollars, have occurred. Tell him of the alarming decline in the value of all property; of the depreciation of all the products of industry; of the stagnation in every branch of business, and of the close of numerous manufacturing establishments, which, a few short months ago, were in active and flourishing operation. Depict to him, if you can find language to portray, the heart-rending wretchedness of thousands of the working-classes cast out of employment. Tell him of the tears of helpless widows, no longer able to earn their bread; and of unclad and unfed orphans, who have been driven, by his policy, out of the busy pursuits in which, but yesterday, they were gaining an honest livelihood.

"Say to him, that if firmness be honorable, when guided by truth and justice, it is intimately allied to another quality of the most pernicious tendency, in the prosecution of an erroneous system. Tell him how much more true glory is to be won by retracing false steps, than by blindly rushing on until his country is overwhelmed in bankruptcy and ruin. Tell him of the ardent attachment, the unbounded devotion, the enthusiastic gratitude toward him, so often signally manifested by the American people, and that they deserve, at his hands, better treatment. Tell him to guard himself against the possibility of an odious comparison, with that worst of the Roman emperors, who, contemplating with indifference the conflagration of the mistress of the world, regaled himself during the terrific scene, in the throng of his dancing courtiers.

"If you desire to secure for yourself the reputation of a public benefactor, describe to him truly the universal distress already produced, and the certain ruin which must ensue from perseverance in his measures. Tell him that he has been abused, deceived, betrayed, by the wicked counsels of unprincipled men around him. Inform him that all efforts in Congress, to alleviate or terminate the public distress, are paralyzed and likely to prove totally unavailing, from his influence upon a large portion of the members who are unwilling to withdraw their support, or to take a course repugnant to his wishes and feelings. Tell him that, in his bosom alone, under actual circumstances, does the power abide to relieve the country; and that, unless he opens it to conviction, and corrects the errors of his administration, no human imagination can conceive, and no human tongue can express the awful consequences which may follow. Entreat him to pause and to reflect, that there is a point beyond which human endurance can not go; and let him not drive this brave, generous and patriotic people to madness and despair."

Who will deny that these were the words of a lofty patriotism,—a patriotism higher than political animosity; higher than disappointed ambition; higher than either revenge for the destruction of a favorite policy, or vindictiveness for personal wrongs. In those eloquent sentences it is not for himself, but for his country, that the noble-hearted orator is pleading.

But the conflict was all in vain. The President, proof against remonstrance; against the evidences of distress; against the censures of Congress, pursued his own inflexible course.

Continually, upon different subjects, the President and the

Senator were coming in conflict. The details of their opposition constitutes largely the exciting history of that period. They were agreed upon scarcely a single measure of foreign or domestic policy. Standing forth as the acknowledged champions of different political creeds, and absorbing, by their commanding positions and striking qualities, the exclusive attention of the public, each seemed to embody in himself the whole executive force of his respective party. Whatever either did possessed the significance, not merely of an individual's action, but of the expression of the will of half a mighty nation. Whenever they came in conflict, it was not as two knights joining in single combat, but as an encounter upon the issue of which were trembling the destinies of two powerful armies.

In 1834, President Jackson, with his characteristic rashness, would have plunged us into a war with France. In the treaty of Paris, 1831, France had agreed to pay the United States twenty-five millions of francs, for aggressions made by that power upon our commerce, during the wars in which she was engaged, from 1800 to 1817. The money was not promptly paid. Jackson, therefore, recommended reprisals upon French property. A war would, of course, have been the result of such a desperate remedy. Mr. Clay interposed to prevent so disastrous a step. As chairman of the committee on foreign relations, he reported a resolution to the effect, "that it was inexpedient at that time, to pass any law, vesting in the President authority for making reprisals upon French property, in the contingency of provision not being made for paying the United States the indemnity stipulated by the treaty of 1831, during the existing session of the French Chambers."

One like Clay, of indomitable courage and Roman firmness, was needed in the Senate Chamber, to curb the headstrong rashness of the Executive. The times, perhaps, demanded a President of the boldness, the decision, the inflexibility of Jackson. But energy like his is, at the same time, eminently dangerous. We can not know what disastrous direction it might have taken, had not Providence, at the critical period, bestowed upon the nation, one capable of holding the strong man in check.

But, among more exciting topics, Mr. Clay did not neglect the calls of philanthropy, nor omit his watchfulness over the financial interests of his country. The oppressed instinctively looked to him for redress of wrongs. His high-toned generosity enjoyed as wide a celebrity as his wonderful eloquence. The poor Indians found in him a defender. The Cherokees, lingering with regretful affection about their old hunting-grounds and the graves of their fathers, were treated with little consideration by the impatient purchasers of their lands. Mr. Clay appeared as their advocate against the people of Georgia. He earnestly deprecated the wanton severity with which the laws of that State were administered against the unfortunate red-men.

Against excessive expenditures, he also interposed his influence. A bill, providing for immense outlays, for the purpose of fortifying our harbors, in view of an apprehended war with France, met with his prompt resistance.

But his position, through those eventful years, was mainly one of conflict. Some of his battles he was compelled to fight over again. The resolution of censure, which, in 1834, the Senate had adopted against President Jackson, Mr. Benton sought to have expunged the following year. The Senate refused, by the decisive vote of thirty-nine to seven. But, two or three years wrought changes in the legislative chambers. In 1837, Mr. Benton renewed the effort, and this time, under circumstances which insured success. Yet Mr. Clay came forward to battle against odds, with the same dauntless spirit with which, three years before, he had battled under the assurance of victory.

"Mr President," he exclaimed, "what patriotic purpose is to be accomplished by this expunging resolution! What new honor or fresh laurels will it win for our common country? Is the power of the Senate so vast, that it ought to be circumscribed, and that of the President so restricted, that it ought to be extended? What power has the Senate? None, separately. It can only act jointly with the other House, or jointly with the Executive. And although the theory of the Constitution supposes that when consulted by him, it may freely give an affirmative or negative response, according to the practice as it now exists, it has lost the faculty of pronouncing the negative monosyllable. When the Senate expresses its deliberate judgment, in the form of resolution, that resolution has no compulsory force, but appeals only to the dispassionate intelligence, the calm reason, and the sober judgment of the community. The Senate has no army, no navy, no patronage, no lucrative offices, nor glittering honors to bestow. Around us there is no swarm of greedy expectants, rendering us homage, anticipating our wishes, and ready to execute our commands.

"How is it with the President? Is he powerless? He is felt from one extremity to the other of this vast Republic. By means of principles which he has introduced, and innovations which he has made in our institutions, alas! but too much countenanced by Congress and a confiding people, he exercises uncontrolled the power of the State. In one hand he holds the purse, and in the other brandishes the sword of the country. Myriads of dependents and partisans, scattered over the land, are ever ready to sing hosannas to him, and to laud to the skies whatever he does. He has swept over the Government, during the last eight years, like a tropical tornado. Every department exhibits traces of the ravages of the storm. Take, as one example, the Bank of the United States. No institution could have been more popular with the people, with Congress, and with State Legislatures. None ever better fulfilled the great purposes of its establishment. But it unfortunately incurred the displeasure of the President; he spoke, and the bank lies prostrate. And those who were loudest in its praise are now loudest in its condemnation. What object of his ambition is unsatisfied? When disabled from age any longer to hold the scepter of power, he designates his successor and transmits it to his favorite. What more does he want? Must we blot, deface, and mutilate the records of the country, to punish the presumptiousness of expressing an opinion contrary to his own?

"What patriotic purpose is to be accomplished by this expunging resolution? Can you make that not to be which has been? Can you eradicate from memory and from history the fact, that in March, 1834, a majority of the Senate of the United

States passed the resolution which excites your enmity? Is it your vain and wicked object to arrogate to yourselves that power of annihilating the past, which has been denied to Omnipotence itself? Do you intend to thrust your hands into our hearts, and to pluck out the deeply-rooted convictions which are there? or is it your design merely to stigmatize us? You can not stigmatize us.

'Ne'er yet did base dishonor blur our name.'

Standing securely upon our conscious rectitude, and bearing aloft the shield of the Constitution of our country, your puny efforts are impotent, and we defy all your power. Put the majority of 1834 in one scale, and that by which this expunging resolution is to be carried in the other, and let truth and justice, in heaven above and on the earth below, and liberty and patriotism decide the preponderance.

"What patriotic purpose is to be accomplished by this expunging? Is it to appease the wrath, and to heal the wounded pride of the chief magistrate? If he be really the hero that his friends represent him, he must despise all mean condescension, all groveling sycophancy, all self-degradation and self-abasement. He would reject with scorn and contempt, as unworthy of his fame, your black scratches, and your baby lines in the fair records of his country. Black lines! Black lines! Sir, I hope the Secretary of the Senate will preserve the pen with which he may inscribe them, and present it to that Senator of the majority whom he may select, as a proud trophy, to be transmitted to his descendants. And hereafter, when we shall lose the forms of our free institutions,—all that now remain to us,—some future American monarch, in gratitude to those by whose means he has been enabled, upon the ruins of civil liberty, to erect a throne, and to commemorate especially this expunging resolution, may institute a new order of knighthood, and confer on it the appropriate name of the 'knight of the black lines.'

"But why should I detain the Senate, or needlessly waste my breath in fruitless exertions? The decree has gone forth. It is one of urgency, too. The deed is to be done; that foul deed, like the blood-stained hands of the guilty Macbeth, all ocean's waters will never wash out. Proceed, then, to the noble work which lies before you, and like other skillful executioners, do it quickly. And when you have perpetrated it, go home to the people and tell them what glorious honors you have achieved for our common country. Tell them that you have extinguished one of the brightest and purest lights that ever burned at the altar of civil liberty. Tell them that you have silenced one of the noblest batteries that ever thundered in defense of the Constitution, and bravely spiked the cannon. Tell them that, henceforward, no matter what daring or outrageous act any President may perform, you have forever hermetically sealed the mouth of the Senate. Tell them that he may fearlessly assume what power he pleases; snatch from its lawful custody the public purse, command a military detachment to enter the halls of the Capitol, overawe Congress, trample down the Constitution, and raze every bulwark of freedom; but that the Senate must stand mute, in silent submission, and not dare to raise its opposing voice. That it must wait until a House of Representatives, humbled and subdued like itself, and a majority of it composed of the partisans of the President, shall prefer articles of impeachment. Tell them, finally, that you have restored the glorious doctrine of passive obedience and non-resistance; and if the people do not pour out their indignation and imprecations, I have yet to learn the character of American freemen."

The lion of the Whig party was now fairly at bay. Upon the field of so many former triumphs in his own proper province, the Senate Chamber, he was at last experiencing defeat. Without, the appearance of his beloved country was in his eyes, to the last degree, deplorable. Contradictory systems of legislation had wrought their disastrous work. Universal depression brooded over all the financial interests of the country. Every newspaper teemed with accounts of new bankruptcies. The fearful times of 1837 are still remembered by business men with shuddering.

The pressure upon the State Banks, where were placed the deposits of the United States Bank, which Jackson had removed, drove Mr. Van Buren, the President, to a new resort. An extra session of Congress was called, to meet in September, 1837. The President, in his message to that body, recommended a system of finance, according to which only gold and silver were to be received by Government, in payment of revenue. The bill, which was reported agreeably to the message, received the name of the Sub-Treasury bill.

Against this Mr. Clay stood forth in strong opposition.

"The great evil under which the country labors," said he, "is the suspension of the banks to pay specie; the total derangement in all domestic exchanges, and the paralysis which has come over the whole business of the country. In regard to the currency, it is not that a given amount of bank-notes will not now command as much as the same amount of specie would have done prior to the suspension; but it is the future, the danger of an inconvertible paper money being indefinitely or permanently fixed upon the people, that fills them with apprehensions. Our great object should be to re-establish a sound currency, and thereby to restore the exchanges, and revive the business of the country.

"The first impression which the measures brought forward by the administration make, is, that they consist of temporary expedients, looking to the supply of the necessities of the Treasury; or so far as any of them possess a permanent character, its tendency is rather to aggravate than alleviate the sufferings of the people. None of them proposes to rectify the disorders in the actual currency of the country; but the people, the States and their banks, are left to shift for themselves, as they may or can. The administration, after having intervened between the States and their banks, and taken *them* into their Federal service, without the consent of the States; after having puffed and praised them; after having brought them, or contributed to bring them into their present situation, now suddenly turns its back upon them, leaving them to their fate! It is not content with that, it must absolutely discredit their issues. And the very people, who were told by the administration that these banks would supply them with a better currency, are now left to struggle as they can, with the very currency which the

Government recommended to them, but which it now refuses itself to receive!

"The professed object of the administration, is to establish what it terms the Currency of the Constitution, which it proposes to accomplish by restricting the Federal Government, in all receipts and payments, to the exclusive use of specie, and by refusing all bank paper, whether convertible or not. It disclaims all purposes of crippling or putting down the banks of the States; but we shall better determine the design or the effect of the measures recommended, by considering them together, as one system.

"The first is the sub-treasuries, which are to be made the depositories of all the specie collected and paid out for the service of the General Government, discrediting and refusing all the notes of the States, although payable and paid in specie.

"Second, a bankrupt law for the United States, leveled at all the State banks, and authorizing the seizure of the effects of any one of them that stops payment, and the administration of their effects under the Federal authority exclusively.

"Third, a particular law for the District of Columbia, by which all the corporations and people of the District, under severe pains and penalties, are prohibited from circulating, sixty days after the passage of the law, any paper whatever not convertible into specie on demand, and are made liable to prosecution by indictment.

"Fourth, and last, the bill to suspend the payment of the fourth installment to the States, by the provisions of which the deposit banks, indebted to the Government, are placed at the discretion of the Secretary of the Treasury.

"It is impossible to consider this system without perceiving that it is aimed at, and if carried out must terminate in, the total subversion of the State banks; and that they will all be placed at the mercy of the Federal Government. It is in vain to protest that there exists no design against them. The effect of those measures can not be misunderstood.

"And why this new experiment, or untried expedient? The people of this country are tired of experiments. Ought not the administration itself to cease with them? ought it not to take warning from the events of recent elections? Above all, should not the Senate, constituted as it is, be the last body to lend itself to further experiments upon the business and happiness of this great people?"

Mr. CLAY opposed to the Sub-treasury scheme, at every stage, the same determined resistance; but, after a hard-fought and protracted contest, after obtaining ground inch by inch, it was carried through both Houses of Congress, and became a law in July, 1840.

Mr. CLAY now stood amid the wrecks of all his proud schemes for the aggrandizement of his country. The Iconoclast, the ruthless image breaker, had passed through them and overthrown them all. His patriotic heart swelled with grief and indignation, as he beheld the desolations of his beloved land. Through years his adversaries had exulted in continual victory. He had been compelled to contemplate, in sorrow, the impotence of his most heroic efforts. Still, through darkness and trial he battled on. The people would awake to their senses, he believed, and better times would come. At last, distant murmurings announced the coming of that looked-for period. The people were rising in their majesty. Hope again sat upon the brow and lighted the eyes of the waiting statesman. How well that hope was justified, and how long the dawning retained its hues of promise, the coming pages will disclose.

CHAPTER XI.

Enthusiasm of 1840—Extra session of Congress—Death of Harrison—Defection of Tyler—Grief of Mr. Clay, at the subversion of his cherished hopes—He advocates a tariff, designed for protection—Resigns his seat—His farewell to the Senate.

Seldom has our country been the scene of such enthusiasm, as that which characterized the Presidential canvass of 1840. The interests of the country, as we have shown, were at the lowest stage of depression. In a change of policy the people fondly hoped to see business revive, and prosperity again smile upon the land. The reaction had fairly come, and in its train, its usual concomitants, extravagant expectations for the future, and almost delirious excitement. Immense mass meetings were held in every part of the country; torchlight processions paraded the streets at night; banners were painted, bearing every possible reference to the hero of Tippecanoe and the Thames; log-cabins were erected, and a sudden passion for "hard cider" seized upon the stoutest advocates of temperance. Such extremes looked almost like madness, but they were the violent rebound of a nation's feelings after years of disaster. The twelve years, during which they had idolized the hero of New Orleans and adhered to his policy, had not brought the promised blessings. Weary with waiting, they rose by a movement almost unanimous, demanding other laws and another order of rulers.

A convention met at Harrisburg. Henry Clay, it was expected, would be their choice; but the American people, in the opinion of the convention, would be more enthusiastic toward a military chieftain. General Harrison received the nomination. Nobly throwing aside every consideration of personal disappointment, Mr. Clay devoted himself to the success of the candidate.

By an immense majority, General Harrison was borne into power.

The new President, as one of his first acts, called an extra session of Congress. The condition of the country demanded, he believed, immediate measures of relief. Congress convened the last day of May, 1841. Meanwhile, President Harrison, to the unutterable grief of the nation, had died. John Tyler, the Vice President, was occupying the Executive Chair. But the country, relying upon the soundness of the men whom it had elevated to power, was yet sanguine and hopeful.

Congress set to work, at once, to repeal the obnoxious laws of previous sessions. The Sub-treasury was abolished. A general bankrupt law was established. A bill to create a National Bank was adopted. Every thing seemed to move on, as the party in power could wish. But suddenly, and from an unexpected quarter, came a check. The Bank bill returned with the President's veto. This announcement fell upon Congress and upon the country like a thunderbolt. The grief and rage of one party and the exultation of the other were extreme. Mr. CLAY, who had entered upon the Session full of spirit, changed his tones from hopefulness to anxiety. When the veto was announced, he arose and addressed the Senate in the following words:

"Mr. President, the bill, which forms the present subject of our deliberations, had passed both Houses of Congress by decisive majorities, and, in conformity with the requirement of the Constitution, was presented to the President of the United States for his consideration. He has returned it to the Senate, in which it originated, according to the direction of the Constitution, with a message announcing his veto of the bill and containing his objections to its passage. And the question now to be decided, is, shall the bill pass by the required Constitutional majority of two-thirds, the President's objections notwithstanding. Knowing, sir, but too well that no such majority can be obtained, and that the bill must fall, I would have been rejoiced to have found myself at liberty to abstain from saying one word on this painful occasion. But the President has not allowed me to give a silent vote. I think, with all respect and deference to him, he has not